Emerging as the
the Right Place at the Right Time:

Leadership in the 21st Century Using The Ellison Model

Problem   Leadership   Solution

ADRIAN N. CARTER
Leadership Development Trainer &
Conflict Resolution Practitioner

ICB PRODUCTIONS, INC
Miami

ISBN-13: 978-1979461849
ISBN-10: 1979461848

ICB Productions, Inc.
P.O. BOX 69-3573 Miami, FL 33269
Printed in the United States of America

www.ICBproductions.net
www.adriancarter.solutions

Dedicated to some of the bridge builders of my life:
Ozzie Ritchey, Dr. Helen Ellison, David Cole, and Dr. Larry Rice

CONTENTS

Foreword by
Mark Rosenberg, Ph.D.
President
Florida International University

Introduction   *1*

Part I: *for the emerging leader*

Chapter 1: The Young & Enthused   *9*
    Personal story
    Being a student leader
    Being a young professional
    Reflective Journal Moment

Chapter 2: Nothing Over Leadership   *21*
    The Organization of Survival
    The Hunt For Success
    Maslow's Hierarchy of Needs
    What Leadership Is
    What Leadership Does
    Reflective Journal Moment

Chapter 3: The Ellison Model   *33*
    The Five Foci
    The Vectors of Conflict
    The Community-Discommunity Circular Diagram
    GOMABCD & The Community Building 7-Step Process
    Hunt's Theorem
    The Ellison Model Principles Associative Graph
    The Ellison Model Techniques
    Keywords of The Ellison Model
    Reflective Journal Moment

Chapter 4: Cole's Leadership-Solution Bridge Concept   *67*
    Types of Leaders
    Followship versus Leadership
    It's Not the Problem That Counts (poem)
    Reflective Journal Moment

Chapter 5: Emerging as the Right Person in the Right Place at the Right Time   *77*
    Right Person, Right Place, Right Time
    Dawn Burgher's Story
    Social Homeostasis
    Tips for the 21st Century Leader
    Reflective Journal Moment

Part II: *for the emerging mentor, advisor, and supervising manager*

Chapter 6: Hunt's Experiential Leadership Process   *91*
    Mentorship
    Hunt's Experiential Leadership Process
    The Ellison Model as a Management Tool
    Customer Service vs. Heart-Felt Service
    Preparing Staff for Work
    Reflective Journal Moment

Part III: *the practitioner*

Chapter 7: Praxis: A Look at The Ellison Model in Play   *107*
    Story #1: K-12 Educator Karen Lundy
    Story #2: Financial Planner Alfredo Alderete
    Story #3: K-12 Educator Nicole Parris-Brown
    Story #4: CPA David Ritchey
    Story #5: Supervisor Tom Ellison
    Story #6: Chef Crystal a "Qui" Harvey
    Story #7: Principal Richard Garrick

Story #8: Aviation Technician Lawrence Darville
Story #9: Charge Nurse Aida Munroe
Story #10: Francina Hosea
Story #11: Operations Supervisor Derrick Lundy Sr.
Story #12: ICB Productions Manager Dexter Hunt
Story #13: Operations Supervisor Alfonso Ritchey
Story #14: Procurement Specialist Jameel Barnes
Story #15: Esquire Deryl G. Hunt, II
Reflective Journal Moment

Chapter 8: The Final Say   *129*
Community Building Anthem
Article of Character

Figure	Description
1	Maslow, A. H. (1954). Maslow's Hierarchy of Needs [Graphic]. Retrieved from Motivation and personality. New York: Harper and Row.
2	Hunt, D. G., Rice, C., and Ritchey, A. (1999). Vectors of Conflict [Graphic]. Retrieved from www.icbproductions.net
3	Hunt, D.G., Rice, C., Ritchey, A., and Carter, A. (2017) Vectors of Perspectives, Diversity, and (Potential) Conflict [Graphic]
4	Carter, A. (2017). Space, Environment, and Relationships Diagram
5	Hunt, D. G. (1999) (2015). The Ellison Model Community-Discommunity Circular Diagram [Graphic]. Retrieved from www.icbproductions.net
6	Hunt, D.G. (2006). GOMABCD: 7-Step Process of Character Development & Community Building [Graphic] The Ellison Model Principles Associative Graph [Graphic]. Adopted from The Ellison Model.
7	Carter, A. (2015a/b/c). The Ellison Model Principles Associative Graph [Graphic]. Adopted from The Ellison Model.
8	Carter, A. (2015). Cole's Leadership-Solution Bridge.
9	Carter, A. (2015). Hunt Experiential Leadership Concept, A Mentor's Guide to Developing Leaders via The Ellison Model [Graphic]. Adopted from The Ellison Model.

MARK ROSENBERG, PH.D.

PRESIDENT OF FLORIDA INTERNATIONAL UNIVERSITY

FOREWORD

When he was asked about how he produced such great dance routines, choreographer Bob Fosse remarked that he always selected "dancers who just don't want to dance but who *gotta* dance." In many ways, this book by Adrian N. Carter is a guide for those who "*gotta* lead" or work with those who lead. Now more than ever, we need to have a more thorough understanding of leadership — what it is, what it is not, its centrality to civil society, and strategies and approaches to nurture leadership.

Carter himself is candid about his own struggle with leadership — how in his youth, his inner instincts of defiance in the face of authority and class peers brought out the worst in him. While he acknowledges that he is neither the first nor the last to make bad decisions, he is pleased of the fact that he has come to grips with how to make better decisions to be more productive and successful. His work pivots around the importance of making and executing the right decisions for the right reasons, attributing much of his turnaround to his college experience at Florida International University in Miami, FL.

The book itself gives considerable attention to The Ellison Model, developed by his mentor Deryl G. Hunt, Ph.D. and named after Helen Ellison, Ed.D., who then served at Florida International University as an assistant vice president. He praises this model because it is an inclusive community building approach that places accountability on leaders at individual, inter-personal and community levels. He then goes on to illustrate how the approach can serve as a "way of life" professionally, socially and personally. The model in essence provides a "tool kit" for making the reader "the right person, in the right place, at the right time — all the time."

This book no doubt fills an important spot in leadership studies because it goes beyond conceptual studies and actually provides personal testimonials from individuals who have used The Ellison Model to bring solutions to the table. But this book is not a one-size-fits-all narrative. It is targeted to student leaders, young professionals, corporate organizations, higher education staff, leadership educators, and life and business coaches, thus giving it a utility that will undoubtedly make it a standard reference for anyone who just doesn't want to lead but who "*gotta* lead!"

Mark B. Rosenberg
President
Florida International University

INTRO
DUCTION

The 21st century presents to us the challenge of building bridges between Baby Boomers and Millennials, a globalized integrated and interactive world through social media and globalization, and at the same time, an increasing amount of diversity amongst people from different socioeconomic, educational, religious, political, geographical, gender, and ethnic backgrounds. How then do we teach leaders how to lead beyond embracing the kaleidoscope of diversity found throughout our society into moving individuals to operate in a mode of inclusion? We have an increasing need for leadership and conflict resolution that not only develops more inclusive leaders who properly embrace the dynamics of our world, but to also combat psychological and physical violence, strengthen coping skills, and raise self-awareness. Moreover, finding new ways to educate and model leadership and conflict resolution approaches to a younger audience of emerging leaders requires innovative voices that can identify with them. Our population of emerging leaders needs effective strategies and a deepened understanding in order to close the loop of diversity that moves from diversity to unity to inclusive community building.

Emerging as the Right Person in the Right Place at the Right Time: Leadership in the 21st Century Using The Ellison Model is a leadership development and conflict resolution book that offers a solution-oriented approach to the question raised above: How do we teach leaders how to lead beyond embracing the kaleidoscope of diversity? The need is meet through the various components of The Ellison Model and other leadership development models created throughout this book. The Ellison Model is a paradigm shifting approach that fosters inclusive community building, strategic planning, program implementation, managing, and personal development as a leader. The major themes of this book include leadership development, mentorship, conflict resolution, inclusion, multicultural appreciation, and relationship building.

This book adds to the epistemological definition of leadership to include the holistic and intrinsic values of The Ellison Model. Readers will understand the components, functionality, and practicality of The Ellison Model; understand conflict resolution as a unitary process; have a broadened definition and understanding of leadership, including why we lead, what leadership does, and how leadership functions; understand how to assess their personal attitude, behavior, communication, and discipline against rubrics for inclusive community building; and understand their responsibility as a mentor in the role of coaching, supervising, and advising. The book offers: 1) an expanded definition of Leadership, 2) information on The Ellison Model 3) a framework with discipline as a core value, 4) a creative approach to leaders mentoring emerging leaders, and 5) approaches to move beyond embracing diversity.

As such, this book is suitable for student leaders, young professionals, higher education administrators, human resource departments for training, and life coaches. It is also ripe for graduate level work in the education and social science fields of study including organizational leadership, educational leadership in both higher education and K-12, public administration, political science, anthropology, criminal justice, human resource management, gender studies, family and marriage counseling, management, public administration, social work, and conflict resolution. Just as important are its uses for corporate training and continuing professional education requirements for supervising managers or aspiring managers.

This book also offers a praxis model, a theoretical and practical framework to assist emerging leaders resolve conflict and build relationships in professional and personal settings. The information on The Ellison Model found throughout the book charges leaders to first reflect on their attitude, behavior, communication and discipline, and assess the ways in which they are impacting their sphere of influence. Firstly, the book speaks to self/inner-development using the Model as a guide. Secondly, the book teaches leaders how to effectively build relationships by reviewing their goal, objective, method, and attitude toward community building. And lastly, the book contains 15 testimonials from professionals from various industries providing real world accounts of the Model in practice.

The information in the book has been class-tested and student tested through a leadership development group I once advised. Named Competitive Edge, this program offered a deepened leadership development experience for student leaders. The students in Competitive Edge received training on the same information presented in the book and were assessed using the model through a project-based curriculum. I was the advisor of Competitive Edge for four years in addition to serving as Director of the department of Student Life & Leadership Development for six years prior in which The Ellison Model was also implemented for student organizations and staff. The model and training components have been used for workshops, seminars, conferences, and staff development trainings. Overall, my training and exposure to The Ellison Model as a trainee and presenter on the model, has offered me great insight over the past 17 years. I have used the model first-hand with the model's creator, Dr. Deryl G. Hunt, at various leadership development and educational events for corporate, government, education, business, and faith-based organizations.

The theoretical framework of The Ellison Model is also designed for studying and building coursework, making it prime for the classroom. The book can be used for instruction in either a combination of traditional and online courses or separately. The chapters contain a light guided-instruction model through the use of reflective questions. The questions are intended to jumpstart self-reflection, class discussions, and may be used as assignments for the students. The book also encourages journaling as a medium for students to reflect on the content. An option to journaling may be the use of electronic responses through other digital platforms such as Blackboard. Because the book is about leadership development and conflict resolution, it's imperative that leaders first and foremost understand who they are and be willing to hold themselves accountable before effectively leading others. Advisors, mentors, and faculty can assess learning outcomes through self-reflection essays; answers to the Reflective Journal Moments & Exercises; project management outlines using The Ellison Model; the student's ability to identify internal conflict; demonstrate current use of themes used throughout the book that students are facing as emerging leaders. Faculty may also use the book for cumulative papers that outline the students' self-reflection, professional goals, areas of growth, and opportunities for development in their management and leadership style. In the corporate setting, supervising managers can assess employee growth through use of The Ellison Model as a project management tool, staff's effectiveness in quality management, and meeting production goals. Advisors and mentors may also use the book as a rubric to assess the intrinsic value of student leadership projects in addition to the external outcomes. The Ellison Model provides components to facilitate this process.

Chapter 1: The Young & Enthused opens up with a personal story of my life as a runaway child trapped in the foster care system. The chapter walks you from my childhood (and the lesson of making poor decisions), to my leadership roles as a student in college, and finally to the importance of transferable skills as a young professional.

Chapter 2: Nothing Over Leadership presents and elaborates on the simple definition of leadership as a survival technique. Using the history of mankind dating back to our hunter-gatherer roots and also using Maslow's Hierarchy of Needs, the chapter further elaborates on leadership and the modes of survival, progress, stagnation, and sense of accomplishment that leaders experience. This chapter also discusses three distinct matters regarding leadership: why we lead, what leadership is, and what leadership does.

Chapter 3: The Ellison Model provides a detailed overview of each Ellison Model component, in addition to elaborating on new concepts that build an expands on the work of the Model creator. The chapter provides rich examples of how each component works collectively and in isolation.

Chapter 4: Cole's Leadership-Solution Bridge Concept presents a new concept for leaders to see themselves as the bridge between a problem/conflict and the solution. The concept was developed and named after my student government advisor David Cole for his reinforcement of solution-oriented leadership.

Chapter 5: Emerging discusses how to become the right person, in the right place, at the right time – all the time. By summarizing the previous chapters (The Ellison Model, the solution bridge, and leadership as an act of survival), the chapter identifies the current theme that flows through each area in establishing the rightness of person, place, and time: Attitude. Encouragingly, the book explains how an individual's attitude is the most significant attribute in the relationship building process, including relationship with self and their sphere of influence.

Chapter 6: Hunt's Experiential Leadership Process (The HELP) introduces a mentorship model to guide managers and supervisors in mentoring emerging leaders. The HELP views leadership as a muscle that needs the right amount of weight, resistance, impact, and repetition in order to stimulate growth and development of the emerging leader. Emerging leaders who ascend to mature leadership must, in return, help to mentor future emerging leaders. Hunt's Experiential Leadership Process, adopted from The Ellison, closes the teaching and learning loop.

Chapter 7: Praxis: A Look at The Ellison Model in Play provides testimonials of professionals from various industries who have successfully used the model. A total of 15 personal stories demonstrating how the five foci of The Ellison Model (inclusion, multicultural appreciation, mentorship, conflict resolution, relationship building) play out in real world situations, including conflict in the workplace and social settings.

Chapter 8: The Final Stay recaps the major points of the book. It also presents two creative works used in plays, songs, and other dramatic performances to reinforce the tenants of The Ellison Model.

The Ellison Model is extremely important to me. It offers a way of life that I fully embrace. Further, The Ellison Model is a paradigmatic shift away from the competitive, dogmatic, and power struggling ways our society teaches and perpetuates. The Ellison Model, an inclusive community building approach to personal and interpersonal interactions, places accountability on leaders at an individual, inter-personal, and community level.

As a conflict resolution practitioner and leadership development trainer with more than 16 years of higher education experience, I choose to help emerging leaders and organizations learn, grow, and develop using The Ellison Model framework. I view The Model as a highly valuable tool kit for helping you become the right person, in the right place, at the right time – all the time! The efficacy of The Ellison Model has accomplished astounding results for more than two decades amongst leaders in local and international governments, businesses, educational institutions, and religious leaders. Additionally, this book adds to the pedagogical forum on leadership development and conflict resolution.

My hope is that you will embrace the principles of this book, *Emerging as the Right Person in the Right Place at the Right Time: Leadership in the 21st Century Using The Ellison Model*, and consequently become a better person, mentor, problem-solver, and leader within your own organization. This book offers a praxis approach to leadership development, conflict resolution, and personal development that when applied can serve as a way of life professionally, socially, and personally. The book will elaborate on the following:

1. Leadership defined at its lowest common denominator

2. An overview of The Ellison Model and its components

3. A 21st century definition of leadership and types of leaders

4. Cole's Leadership-Solution Bridge Concept

5. The Three R's and how to be the Right Person, in the Right Place, at the Right Time

6. The Hunt Experiential Leadership Concept, an integrated Ellison Model approach to leadership development training for mentors

7. A Look at The Ellison Model in Practice: Personal testimonials from leaders who have used The Ellison Model to develop solutions

Part I
for the emerging leader

THE YOUNG & ENTHUSED

Chapter 1

"I feel my heart glow with an enthusiasm which elevates me to heaven, for nothing contributes so much to tranquillize the mind as a steady purpose — a point on which the soul may fix its intellectual eye." – "Frankenstein" by Mary Shelley, 19th century English novelist.

I watched my stepmother through the back window of the house zip around in the kitchen. She walked from the counter to the microwave, back to the counter, and back to the microwave. Then her thick arms, with a long silver-serving spoon, moving like a crane between tall buildings, would come up, move over to what must have been a plate, and then back down into the pot. Her intense focus to put the right amount of rice, or maybe it was peas and mashed potatoes, could not go unnoticed. I would never know what was served for dinner that night.

Earlier that day during lunch, my fist met the face of an antagonizing classmate. The cafeteria hummed with chatter and random outburst of laughter. Kids had tooth-stained smiles from bag lunches their mom had prepared. I was one of those kids. Secretly, I loved the peanut butter and jelly sandwiches my stepmom prepared for me weekly. However, as much as possible I tried to hide what I was eating. Not all of my classmates enjoyed watching me eat my peanut butter and jelly sandwich. My lunch was often met with some sly remark from a classmate or two who had somehow determined that brown paper bags and PB&J were the hallmark of kids whose parents did not have a lot of money. Somehow, in defense of my sandwich, I found myself standing in the middle of the cafeteria swinging my arms like a windmill on the windiest of days trying to punch this kid in his face. My classmate swung back the best way any fourth grader knew how. We eventually swung ourselves right into the assistant principal's office.

That was my third fight for the school year. The assistant principal did not suspend me from school for this fight. They did not even call my parents. They told me something worse: I could not return to school without my parents coming with me (insert surprise face emoji). They put the entire ordeal in my hands to communicate to my parents. It scared the crap out of me. I imagined thirty different ways this scenario could play out, but they always came back to one conclusion. I knew I was going to be in grave trouble. North Glade Elementary School was my second school that year. Prior to that I was attending Greynolds Park Elementary School where I had also gotten into trouble for cursing at another student. Now, here I was, against my parent's best advice and attempts to guide me, in trouble at school again. How do I explain that I fought over a peanut butter and jelly sandwich? Maybe this is why later on throughout middle and high school I always found it difficult to bring myself to fight another student – there was never a good enough reason. But I knew when my parents got home after 6 p.m. that it was going to be a long night.

The moon cracked through the leaves as I crouched next to the storage shed and behind the hedges that lined the backyard fence. It was a tight fit and it was a little prickly from the twigs and leaves. As I tried to find a firm place for my feet and knee, I wrestled with the thought of toughing it out, walking into the house and just telling my parents what happened. But I had decided the only solution to this problem was to run away from home. I thought about it more as I watched my stepmother through the back window. I changed my mind, and then changed my mind again. I wondered if she would realize I wasn't in the house. I am sure my plate went cold that night. I decidedly crept slowly from the backyard, out the front driveway, and hurried to the bus stop.

I did not have any bus fare, but I stepped into my getaway car with full hopes of talking my way into a free ride. But the bus driver did not seem to care too much. He let me onto the bus, which was bright like daytime on the inside, as the eyes of the world seemed to shut on the outside of the bus as the driver closed the door. I remembered how to get back to my aunt's old neighborhood, which wasn't too far from my old best friend's house in North Miami Beach. His name was Lee. He had a Nintendo game system with the larger controller. At the time, I thought that was the coolest thing ever. His mom was nice and used to let me come by and play video games with him every once in a while. I used to hike from the apartments to my aunt's house, and then to Lee's house one block away. This would be my first time visiting Lee in months since my family and I had moved from the Avalon Apartments. Now here I was standing at their door. I knocked. His mother answered. We were both surprised.

I was invited in to sit and explain how I made it to her house at this time of night. I told her what had happened in school earlier that day, and that I was scared to go home because I knew my stepmom was going to beat me. But my recount of my stepmom did not stop there. I talked about other instances in which she was heavy-handed. I told her enough to raise her cause for concern. She called my parents thereafter, but she also called the police. The story took a different turn when the cops arrived. I thought I was going to go home and finally get to see what was served for dinner that night, but that certainly was not the next turn of events.

I was turned over to the Human Resource Services (HRS), now known as the Department of Children and Family (DCF). I was brought to their office and seated in a cubicle area with an older woman to rehash the day's event all over again. They placed me in a shelter tucked into the corner of a Miami Gardens neighborhood off 37th avenue and north of 199th street. It was in walking distance to my now new school, North Carol City Elementary. The school was later renamed after my principal, Barbara Hawkins, who had died in a car accident several years later.

The shelter was filled with a pair of bunk beds in each room and plenty of other kids around my age. I did a lot of jumping from one top bunk to the other. That was the most fun parts of my day. The other part of my day was often filled with writing poetry about running away, family, and love. I may have only been nine years old, but I remember the poetry being so deep that I had to throw them away. I told myself this could not be my life to write this much pain into a poem. Each time I read my own writing I was taking back further into disbelief.

It was getting close to the holidays and families from the community would visit and interact with us. One couple took particular interest in me. I cannot recall if they were married or not, but they seemed to really empathize with me. There was a special event day with a bunch of visitors who came with gifts for the kids. This couple brought me the biggest box of toys and games – a bigger box than what any other kid had received that day. It was overwhelming and I quietly felt so undeserving. Mixed with feelings of excitement and uneasiness, I remember the distance I had in my mind. I was present in body, but absent in my heart.

I do no know what triggered it, but I somehow grew with resentment for the shelter and decided again that running away would be the best thing to do. With just the clothes on my back and nightfall pending, I walked out the gate and headed down the street; occasionally looking back to see if anyone had noticed I was gone. The police picked me up hours later after I wandered around the neighborhood. Turns out I did not make it that far. I was again returned to HRS and seated in a cubicle, telling them how much I did not like the shelter. This time they placed me into a foster home.

The foster home family was very nice to me. The house was a medium size home in a Miami neighborhood near 135th street and the busy intersection of either 441 or 27th avenue. The house had a lot of brown furniture and dimly lit rooms. I do no recall a man in the home, just an older senior lady with all her faculties and her lady friend who always visited. At times there were one or two other foster kids in the home. We went to church every Sunday and she spoke encouragingly to us. She had an ironed-in front porch on which I used to sit and play Twinkle-Twinkle Little Star on my little, black Casio keyboard.

I liked the teacher at my newest elementary school – my fourth school that year. It was down the street from the foster home. But my classmates weren't so fond of me. I noticed a poster on the wall in my classroom that said Shaka of the Zulus. But when we talked about the Zulus, Shaka was referred to as Shaka Zulu. I was slightly confused. So I asked my teacher to clarify if his name was Shaka Zulu or Shaka of the Zulus. I was told later on the basketball court during P.E., as two kids approached me with balled fists, that I asked too many questions in class. That experience confused me dramatically and for a lot of years it made learning uncomfortable. It wasn't until I got to college that I felt appreciated for having an inquisitive mind. But on that basketball court, nine years old, I could not rationalize how asking a question, in class, at school – a place of learning – was problematic. I can remember standing on the court with a puzzled face asking them the same question over and over as they made their threats.

"So, you wanna fight me cause I asked a question," I asked them.

"It was time to go to P.E. and you kept on talking," they replied.

"So, you wanna fight me cause I asked a question," I asked again.

"It was time to go."

"But we're in school. To learn."

And the back and forth continued as the other students looked on like it was tennis match. Within a couple months I ran away from the foster home. I really wanted to go back home to my stepmom and dad. I wanted to make up for the meals I had missed. So I took off in the middle of the day on a Saturday and made my way to a very busy 135th street. I felt so confused. It was hot. I could hear the heat roaring from the cars, the dry air seeping from the street, and the sun lashing across my forehead. I was looking for shade as much as I was looking for a way home.

I made it to a pay phone and called where I used to call home. My stepmom answered. She was elated to hear from me. She arrived 30 minutes later in my father's black two-door Toyota. She hugged me and never had I been happier to see her. However, she knew she could not hold on to me and had to inform my social worker of my whereabouts. So again I went back to the shelter I was originally placed in. I also went back to North Carol City Elementary.

The shelter proved too unsettling. There was one particular counselor who seemed intolerable of me. She told me plainly I was just a rude, stubborn boy who did not want to listen. Her words had merit. But her directness made me uncomfortable. I found myself walking out the gate again and down the street refusing to return. The police officer found me in an open field of dead grass and sand, sitting on a rock near a broken fence with the shelter off in the distance behind me. The only thing I did was sit, think, and draw circles with my feet and a broken tree branch. The officer calmly talked to me and encouraged me to come with him. This time around HRS chose to place me with the closest relative in the family. The problem with that was that I did not have any close extended family members. Alternatively, I was placed with a family from our church.

I did not return to my parents for over six months. In the meantime, as I moved between shelter and foster homes, my parents were pulled into counseling services and had to complete mandatory parenting classes in order to regain custody of me. I did not find this out from my parents until I was well into my 30s. After having my own kids is when it became unfathomable to think of the amount of pain and concern a parent can experience from their child running away and being in the government's custody.

As you see, each decision to run was a decision to jump from the pot into the fire. Being in the custody of HRS only resulted in me being moved between multiple foster homes and shelters, each time switching the elementary school I attended. The wrong answer to a problem had set me on a course of more problems for my parents and myself. I may have only been nine years old, but I can clearly remember a voice that spoke to me that night as I knelt down behind the hedges at the back of my parent's house. It said to me, "You don't have to do this." My failure to listen suppressed the leader in me and resurrected an attitude of defiance. It took years to rebound from that decision.

Fortunately, I've come a long way since the age of nine. I lacked self-management and accountability as a young adult. However, I am totally a product of my environment. My mentors consisted of a handful of people including my parents, teachers, professors, and spiritual leaders who took an interest in my success. These individuals mentored me to a place where my outlook, attitude, behavior, and discipline began to align with my purpose. I count my experiences all joy because they have brought me to this point in life, the opportunity to reflect and present to you steps on growing and developing into the right person in the right place at the right time for the dispensation of the 21st century.

My experiences at nine-years old and growth in adulthood are not necessarily different from the way in which our governmental, educational, business, and religious leaders make decisions. What they do today will possibly have a lifetime impact on themselves and the communities they serve. Likewise, what YOU do will have a lasting impact, whether good, bad or ugly. Decisions are powerful because they carry rewards and consequences that can last a lifetime. I am not the first or the last to have made poor decisions. I am also not the first, nor will I be the last, to have learned how to make better decisions and be a more productive and successful person in society.

Emerging as the Right Person in the Right Place at the Right Time is about learning how to make and execute the right decisions in your life for the right reasons. It is important to eventually move from that nine-year-old runaway into a leader who emerges into the lives of people to provide leadership and hope. After many years of struggle, many of which I was the only one privy to, I found the better parts of myself as a leader when I arrived to college.

Being A Student Leader

College provided an expanded view of the world that I had never experienced before. Asking questions in a college classroom demonstrated inquisitiveness and a desire to learn – something professors and other students were almost always supportive of. College classrooms are usually filled with active learners who reward your curiosity. Unlike the kids on the basketball court when I was nine-years-old, this time my classmates approached me after class with open arms lobbying me to join their study group. It turns out I was really good at finite math.

I began college the summer of 1999 at one of the largest institutions in Miami, Florida. The satellite campus where I took all of my classes for my broadcast journalism major was small and quaint, yet the communities of people quickly made it feel nostalgic. I could tell the incoming freshmen and the students who had already been there really enjoyed the atmosphere. It may have been the welcome back parties we had – there were several – or the bay that flowed to the back of our campus from Biscayne. It was serene, beautiful, and almost unbelievable that our campus was built around a natural body of water. On the other hand, it may have been the staff. After all, the people of organizations are everything. The staff proved to be very helpful, especially employees from The Office of Multicultural Programs and Services, The International Student Office, and the Recreation Department. Additionally, the faculty and their intentions to be rigorous were very evident. But it was something – a combination of a lot of things required to make the University function properly.

My most unfortunate experience was the amount of times I had to resubmit my high school transcript – four times to be exact before meeting all of the admission requirements. I remember the annoyance. I handed them a copy, reiterated that this was my third time submitting it to them, and I still had to get a fourth one turned in. However, in hindsight, I am happy that that was the worst of it. It could have been a hold on my financial aid preventing payment for the semester – and nobody likes his or her money being played with. So I'll be gentle with my complaint about the high school transcript. I quickly grew with great affinity for the University. It became a home away from home. Between the staff, the bay, the buildings, the faculty, and the sheer excitement of being accepted into a quality university, I was enthusiastic and ambitious about my academic future.

I met the Student Government vice president during new student orientation. She doubled as a peer advisor for incoming freshmen students, giving campus tours and informing them about the types of services available on campus. Later during the fall semester she told me about a vacancy for the coordinator of a spirit group run through the Student Government called Panther Power. I worked a job off campus during my first semester, but I considered the convenience of going to school and working in the same place. I started frequenting the Student Government office and eventually became the Panther Power coordinator the Spring semester of my freshmen year. It quickly became more than just a matter of convenience. It was an opportunity for personal development that I never knew existed. I later went on to serve as the Student Government vice president followed by two consecutive terms as president of the FIU Biscayne Bay Campus. I even ran unopposed for my second term.

The opportunities I had as coordinator, vice president, and president were tremendous. By the time I graduated with my bachelors in journalism and mass communications, I had coordinated over 50 events on campus and had served on multiple university committees. I had served on the university wide activity and service fee allocation committee each of my four years. This committee in particular allocated up to $7 million for Student Affairs programs and services. I also served as budget manager of a half-a-million-dollar operational budget, fundraised thousands of dollars for international student scholarships, and sat on the university's foundation board. Additionally, I served on multiple search and screen committees for the hiring of high-level administrators. I even led a march to the Florida capitol in Tallahassee as we rallied against proposed changes to the Bright Future's Scholarship Program run through the state of Florida.

David Cole, the associate director for campus life, was an excellent student advisor who constantly empowered me with words of affirmation and reflective conversations. Cole showed me how to build excellent relationships with the university administrators including the University President, vice president of student affairs, the provost, and other important leaders in the University. He taught me how to prepare for meetings, be aware of the issues, and to seek feedback from the constituency I served, the student body.

I learned how to represent the student body by being direct but respectful. This process often called for me to challenge the status quo of the University. I once sat in a meeting with faculty and the vice president of student affairs as they discussed a new initiative they wanted to implement. While I liked the new initiative, however, I observed a double standard in how decisions were being made at the University. "When the university wants to do something we talk about our need to be innovative and groundbreaking," I shared aloud. "But when the administration doesn't want to do something, the students are told that is not the way the university does things." My comments were surprisingly well received and raised further discussion in the meeting from other faculty members and administrators. I disliked the way certain administrators justified their agenda and did not prioritize the things Student Government felt were also important. However, that is people and politics in a nutshell no matter where you go; It is part of the process. I understood this better as I grew as a professional.

My success as a student leader was not my own. My immersed experience was always housed in The Ellison Model being developed by my mentor,

Sociologist Deryl G. Hunt, Ph.D. Dr. Hunt had began creating the early parts of the Model while working at Florida International University as the Associate Director of Multicultural Programs & Services. In addition to Dr. Hunt, I was fortunate enough to have several mentors in the University throughout my undergraduate years including David Cole, Associate Vice President of Student Affairs Dr. Helen Ellison, and Multicultural Programs and Services Coordinator Ozzie Ritchey. Outside of the University, Johnson and Wales University (JWU) Vice President of Academic Affairs Dr. Larry Rice also played a pivotal role in my life. Dr. Rice now serves as president of JWU North Miami Campus. This book is dedicated to Cole, Ellison, Ritchey, and Rice.

Being a Young Professional

As a young professional coming out of college, my vivid imagination of success ensured me that a big paying job was right around the corner waiting to embrace me with open arms. I skipped down that road whistling I thought that I was going to come out of college and land a big paying job. After all, I had a college degree. Isn't that what they told you all through grade school: go to college and then you will get a good paying job. They showed you statistics that people with a higher education made more money than those with only a high school diploma. Well, I had to learn – the hard way – that It is true, to an extent. The extent varies depending on your field of study, and usually, the payoff comes after gaining some experience. I remember being turned down for a job for not having enough experience. I was puzzled. How do I gain experience if no one hires me? Nonetheless, I learned that having a higher education degree does provide a higher payout, in the long run – and that is the part they did not tell you. It is not an immediate pay out. In fact, there are plenty of multi-millionaires without a college degree.

Not finding the kind of job I wanted after graduating with my bachelors was a little disheartening. I had completed my bachelor's degree in journalism, but I already knew that wasn't the field I wanted to practice in. I was turned off from journalism after realizing that objectivity was subjectively defined. In my youthful idealism, I thought news was the one altruistic stop we had on this city bus of life. Additionally, I considered politics. My tremendous involvement and exposure to State politics made a political career seem ideal. However, my first job out of college was as an administrative assistant for the non-profit organization of the former Miami Dolphins football player Nat Moore.

I eventually interviewed for a coordinator's position in student affairs at a local community college. I had decided to pour back into higher education with all of my student affairs experience as a student. As I grew professionally, I could not help but recognize (and appreciate) my learning experience as a student leader on campus. My experiential learning at the university armed me with so many skills that were transferable to my professional job. I felt empowered entering the professional workforce. As a young professional, I had brought a lot of leadership and creativity to the table. However, I soon realized that I had a lot to learn.

After a year and half at the college, I moved from being the assistant director to the director of the Department of Student Life and Leadership Development. Similar to my student government days, I found myself managing over a half-million dollar operational budget, supervising five full-timers and over 30 part-timers, sitting in on committee meetings, and coordinating events. As a professional, I was not as outspoken. I quickly learned tact, and in general, understood the parameters of being employed by a company did not carry the same flexibility as being in student governance.

I had an excellent mentor and supervising manager in David Ascensio, the Dean of Student Affairs. He taught me how to manage a professional staff, choose my battles more wisely, and most importantly, how to identify the most important parts of my role that were both tangible and intangible. He also taught me how to navigate within the organization.

My professional success was not my own. The Ellison Model had grown to be an intricate part of my life. I was a growing product of the model. I had been trained in the model and had trained on the model locally, nationally, and internationally. I managed my departments using the model and trained my staff on it. I even conducted professional development for the organization on the model.

Whether a student leader or a young professional in your career, we all operate under a certain model. Whether learned from our parents, religious institution, best friend, television characters, experiences, or a combination of them all, some moral compass deeply and profoundly guides us on a daily basis. I believe most, if not all people, want to learn and grow to a better version of themselves. As a result, you learn that one of the most important things you do is learn and apply. And what you learned yesterday can change tomorrow. But again, you learn and apply and repeat as necessary until its perfected in your daily living.

Reflective Journal Moment

1. Write your personal story about a critical part of your life and identify any patterns of destructive behavior.

2. Create a list of key people who have helped you grow into the person you are today. Next, select a person from your list and write a thank you letter to them. Be sure to explain to them the obstacles you faced and the role they played in helping you overcome.

NOTHING

OVER

LEADERSHIP

Chapter 2

"I had no epiphany, no singular revelation, no moment of truth, but a steady accumulation of a thousand slights, a thousand indignities and a thousand unremembered moments produced in me an anger, a rebelliousness, a desire to fight the system that imprisoned my people. There was no particular day on which I said 'Henceforth I will devote myself to the liberation of my people;' instead, I simply found myself doing so, and could not do otherwise." – Nelson Mandela, South African anti-apartheid revolutionary, political leader, and philanthropist, who served as President of South Africa

No other earthbound entity is more pre-occupied with human beings than human beings. Humans people-watch; give updates on one another's interactions to others; voice opinions on how people should conduct themselves; mirror the behavior of others; create cliques (in-groups and out-groups); challenge people's abilities and intellect; and make assumptions about how people should think, act, and feel. Humans are social beings and seek euphoria through interactions with other human beings. There's nothing wrong with that because among our greatest euphoric experiences as humans is witnessing the success of others. Even those who appear to dislike or are unsupportive of another's success, still acknowledge success. In truth, it is the success of someone else that gives us hope and confirms the human ability for us to be personally successful. It signals to us that we too have a chance. After all, if someone else did it, we can do it too.

Watching someone become successful is one thing. To be a part of the reason for a person's success is another. Because human beings enjoy being a part of other human being's success, they have set up structured entities such as governmental agencies, organizations, and corporations to assess and manage the success stories of others. In the process of structuring entities to manage success, and in the spirit of being people watchers, we subsequently created leadership as a field of study in order to further assess, manage, learn, and teach how to more effectively and efficiently achieve the success a particular agency is striving toward. Success is usually considered a result of effective leadership. Moreover, in a society of professionals, experts, idealists, and perfectionists, individuals often have a desire to hold someone accountable for the success or failure of a goal. The patting on the back or finger pointing is a heightened pre-occupation with the study of human behavior that has subsequently culminated into what we call leadership.

Leadership contains numerous definitions by various theorists and practitioners, including businessmen and women, educators, psychologists, and sociologists. By these definitions, leadership involves, but are not limited to the following: helping; serving; influencing; inspiring; empowering; training; and equipping individuals Leadership, regarded by some as an art form, is also knowing when to be out front regarding an issue; when to be behind the scenes; demonstrating character and humility; setting the example; being a visionary; and learning to actively listen. All of these definitions are correct in some form or another. Throughout our growth and development, we discover that leadership shows up in a number of ways depending on whom you are serving, managing, directing, supervising, or partnering.

Leadership is often branded as going against the grain, taking initiative, or standing out from the in-crowd. In reality, standing apart from the popular voice is more of a by-product of leadership, and not leadership in and of itself. Leadership has also become a marketing platform for many speakers, trainers, and coaches who have chunked down leadership into a certain number of steps or series of letters, such as 'three-steps' to this or the 'A-B-C's' of that. Just as standing apart from the popular voice does not wholly define leadership; neither do these steps and acronyms. Instead, they help us to remember the components of leadership. While leadership includes all of the above definitions and works in the various capacities mentioned, they do not tell us *why* we lead. The *why* tells us what motivates leadership. The answer to *why* also helps us to identify whether leadership is innate or learned, a constantly debated question in the field of leadership. Let's first discuss *why* we lead, followed by what leadership is and what leadership does.

Why We Lead: The Organization of Survival

Leadership, in its most primal form, at its lowest common denominator is simply a survival technique. Human beings lead in order to survive. Furthermore, the desire to survive is innate, and how to survive is taught, even if it means teaching ourselves. Survival of self, whether physical, emotional, spiritual, financial, or biological is the single most important motivation for the human being. The steps we take in leading, which may include communicating, taking initiative, networking, teambuilding, mobilizing others, and influencing others is always for the purpose of our most innate purpose, to survive and in the process of surviving, live as emotionally, physically, and spiritually comfortable as possible.

From the very beginning, human beings have taken leadership as a mode of survival and self-preservation. Let's consider the Paleolithic era of hunting and gathering from nearly 10,000 years ago. When food was hard to come by for the hunter-gatherer, they devised more effective strategies to hunt and capture food. They figured out a way to set traps, turn a rock into a blade, camouflage, and do the necessary for a single purpose: survive. In today's language we will say they used analytics, strategic planning, mass production, and essentially, best practices to move their organization of survival forward. As the caveman developed, these skills and strategies were taught to one another through oral and written tradition, practiced, and inculcated throughout generations. And in true human fashion, each generation has improved upon the process. Surviving and progressing are what we do.

The Hunt for Success

Effective leadership results in growth and development for individuals and communities. It can be seen as **progress**. Progress invigorates the human spirit and makes us feel alive. It is movement, action, and interaction that bring about a **sense of accomplishment**. In progress we find ambition, creativity, innovation, and most importantly, solutions. We measure success by progress. On the other hand, **stagnation** is demotivating and unfulfilling. Stagnation attempts to kill the drive to learn, innovate, and solve. Stagnation in an individual's life causes a reaction of flight (running from the challenge) or fight (engaging in the process to overcome and grow to the next level). This reminds me of the adage, "You don't go through, you grow through." Most individuals desire progress over stagnation (life over death), even in their most stagnate position, by taking leadership or expecting those in leadership positions to help move them forward. If not, hopes, dreams, and promises diminish (or die) for individuals and their communities. What is important about the *need* to survive is ensuring that an inclusive community building approach, and not just personal gain, motivates the individual toward progress.

No different from our hunter-gatherer instinct, individuals hunt for success by taking the necessary leadership to survive and avoid "dying" in a position of stagnation. To reiterate, leadership is the organization of survival. We survive to live, and we live by making progress. We measure survival through our **sense of accomplishment**. Our sense of accomplishment is: 1) a powerful tool of motivation for taking leadership, and 2) a reward we internally give ourselves for the progress we've made. And as best practices for survival have been passed on for over 10,000 years, leaders always want to leave an impression after they are gone. What will they say about you after you have graduated from the institution, moved to another department, or gotten hired at another company? Our character and integrity as leaders establishes our credibility or lack thereof; it establishes our **legacy**. The legacy of your parents lives on through your birth – a reflection of how we biologically survive. Leaders, such as Martin Luther King, Jr., live on through legislation passed by the United States government due to his efforts during the Civil Rights movement. The life work of Nelson Mandela, Marcus Garvey, the Dalai Lama, Maya Angelou, Shakespeare, and other notables have continued to impact our lives long after they are gone. Similarly, your legacy is the impact you have on your community or organization. Our sense of accomplishment becomes our legacy, even if we are the only one who knows it, even if unbeknownst to us. Our existence in the 21st century is the legacy of the hunter-gatherers.

Leadership According to Maslow's Hierarchy of Needs

Abraham Maslow's (1987) Hierarchy of Needs succinctly demonstrates how human beings take leadership for the single purpose of survival. The hunter-gatherer may have been pre-occupied with just living. Over time, like all things, we grow and develop and want more and better for ourselves. Do you remember what happened after you pleaded for that one toy, promised your parents that is all you wanted for your birthday, and promised to be well-behaved for it? You got the toy. You were over-joyed, and within a short span of time, you wanted a new toy. What were toys for us as children are now goals for us as adults. New goals equal new challenges and higher aspirations. We've moved from wanting a new bike that shifts gears to wanting a new car that shifts gears. Similarly, we go from just wanting to get our foot into the door with a company to wanting a promotion, bigger pay, and possibly a bigger office. Simply put, sometimes we outgrow our current station in life and need something new to invigorate our creativity.

Maslow (1999) states it best when he shares that "Growth takes place when the next step forward is subjectively more delightful, more joyous, more intrinsically satisfying than the previous gratification which we have become familiar and even bored." Think about the feeling you have when you feel stuck in your current situation, whether in terms of the position you have at work, the amount of finances you have been able to garner, or even the academic program you have been pursuing. That feeling is very unsettling and often hard to shake until you make some degree of progress.

Let's examine the typology to analyze how we make progress through our varying life circumstances. After an individual's physiological needs are met, he or she intrinsically desires to ensure his or her safety through employment, a moral compass for internal guidance, reliability from immediate family, and the comfort of being healthy enough to come and go freely. As it appears, the physiological and safety needs provide stability for our emotional and physical health. After which, we can then attempt to more rewardingly build external relationships in order to establish a heightened sense of love and belonging. Accordingly, the additional needs in the pyramid become a focal point after we grow familiar, content, or, as previously mentioned, bored with our current level of achievement.

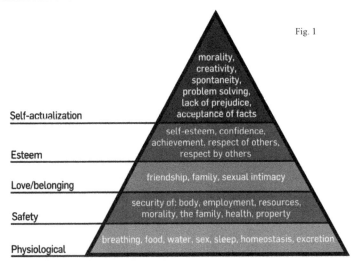

Fig. 1

Now that your basic needs and support systems are intact, the question becomes, "What's next?" Put another way, how does an individual move to the next level of achievement to ascertain a sense of actualization as their authentic self? Answer: they take the necessary leadership to ascertain it. The emptiness from feeling unfulfilled in one area of Maslow's typology is what people try to avoid. The desires for more becomes a part of an individual's internal struggle to survive. If a person does not have proper food and shelter, their initial motivation would be to overcome that challenge before being concerned with being a CEO of a company. Similarly, the person who has held a certain position for five years may feel as if they are not growing or progressing in the position. Ascertaining a newer or higher position may be their only satisfaction. In another scenario, an individual may not feel accomplished until they have completed their academic program. The leadership they implement to achieve a sense of accomplishment may vary across the board. But the fuel to "survive" their state of stagnation is a powerful motivator to deploy leadership.

Accordingly, as a person completes one level of Maslow's Hierarchy of Needs, they develop a certain level of motivation to evolve into the next need. In other words, survival is not only a physical pursuit, as it relates to our ability to breathe, reason, and have full working functions of our body. Survival in this book speaks to the holistic person, inclusive of the emotional, psychological, financial, biological, spiritual, physical space, and socio-economic life that we each possess. In all aspects of life, individuals take effective leadership in an effort to survive.

Maslow's research on the developmental process most importantly establishes a hierarchy based on *needs*. These are milestones in the growth and development process that human beings achieve in order to feel and live as a physically, emotionally, and spiritually complete person. Anything short of these needs may leave an individual feeling insufficient or outright unfulfilled.

What Leadership Is

People often intertwine what leaders do versus who leaders are. However, the combination of the two gives us leadership. We can splice leadership as: 1) a standalone organism that defines **what leadership is,** and 2) the combination of what leadership is and the practice of the individual leader to define **what leadership does**. For example, someone's occupation tells us what he or she does, not who they are. To know who they are tells us *how* they do what they do. Put another way, to know who they are reveals the character of the individual from which we can surmise *how* they perform their job. For example, an individual may practice accounting (the *what*), but are they trustworthy (the *how*)? In addition to leadership being a survival technique, let's further examine what leadership is and then examine what leadership does.

Leadership is a living, breathing organism that requires the right environment for its sustainability. Like any organism, when leadership does not get the proper nutrients from its host, its capacity to function at its highest potential is greatly diminished. Additionally, like any organism, leadership fights for survival by any means necessary. All living things fight to live. Life brings forth life, essentially serving as its own catalyst for survival. Leadership is a living, breathing organism that exists in every human being. In other words, everyone in some form or another contains the capacity to lead. You, as a leader, are the host of this living, breathing organism that requires the right environment for growth and development. Intuitively, something in you fights to remain alive beyond your physical presence and is manifested through the legacy you build. The better of a host you are to the leadership development process, the better of a leader you become. At the micro level the individual, such as you, serves as the host. At the macro level the mentor serves as the host. Let's dissect this further.

The **micro** level deals with you and what you feed yourself for the sustainability of your leadership development. These are the personal steps you take to support your growth. For example, what is your self-talk? Do you feed yourself words that say you cannot or that you are incapable? Do you give enough effort just to get by? Are you under-confident? Are you overconfident? Do you pretend to be someone you are not--faking it until you make it? Do you sabotage your own success? I purposely asked the questions in this manner to cause self-reflection, paying special attention to the negative side of our self-talk or ways we falsify our identity to ourselves. Only through an honest, transparent relationship with ourselves can we properly host this living, breathing organism called leadership.

At the **macro** level, the mentor serves as the host of your leadership development. Mentorship is always experienced through a person, including the places and things they create. Individuals or groups of people create places, whether physical or digital. Similarly, individuals or groups create things, evidenced through technology and information. People are always part of the process of creating, innovating, or establishing other people, places, and things. People mentor people; the places created by people mentors people;

and the things created by people also mentor people. Places may also include the organizational environment, which may potentially impact how you feel about a particular person, place or thing.

Places and things are always reflective of the attitude and character of the persons who shaped them. Places that mentor you includes the college and university, your old or current neighborhood, the company or organization for which you work, the overall community, and city, town, or county governance through its rules and regulations and modes of law enforcement. Your favorite television show can be your mentor. By embracing the values of the television character, even an animated character, you can be mentored into thought processes and behaviors that steer the way you live your life. In fact, people often embrace the persona of fictional characters to symbolize their strength or aptitude. Characters such as Superman, Rocky, the Godfather, Wonder Woman, Brotha' Man from the Fifth Flo, and the ladies from Sex in the City are a few that come to mind. We do the same for athletes and celebrities. At the end of the day, whether fictional or not, these characters are people or have the persona of people, such as the talking teacup and candlestick holder in the Disney animated film, Beauty and the Beast, and ultimately impacts the way we see ourselves and the world and the ways in which we behave. Yet, our more direct mentors come by way of our supervising managers, seasoned colleagues, academic advisors, and other notables in our field of study. They also come by way of people who share our interest. Accordingly, we use their teaching material such as books, podcasts, or websites to mentor us. Mentors who work directly with us to host our leadership development process work to inspire, challenge, and encourage us toward becoming more effective leaders.

What Leadership Does

Leadership often starts from your waking position in bed before you ever set foot on the ground. While lying in bed, the mind begins to make goals for the day by mapping out a schedule, prioritizing events, determining whose callbacks are important or urgent. We often times utilize affirming words of encouragement to motivate getting out of bed and start making progress.

Ultimately, every decision we make is an act of leadership. Whether this is a poor or plausible act of leadership may not be known at the time. Nonetheless, despite whether the goal is major or minor, people do what they feel they must in order to progress and achieve success, thereby providing themselves with a sense of accomplishment. There is a personal satisfaction associated with every accomplishment, even when the intent or goal was achieved for someone besides one's self. As I've pointed out, starting from your waking position, what leadership does is **take action** by envisioning and executing goals that progresses the individual and their sphere of influence toward success. As we learn more about The Ellison Model in the next chapter, we will come to understand how its methodologies are an effective approach to simultaneously mobilize the community at large toward survival/progress while also moving ourselves forward as a member of the same.

Leadership is a **conglomerate of skills** set in motion to fulfill a goal or purpose. What leadership does is effectively execute any of these skills at the appropriate time. These skills include effective written and verbal communication, taking initiative, organizing, time management, negotiating, analyzing, synthesizing, delegating, being proficient with technology, actively listening, problem solving, having intellectual and emotional intelligence, envisioning, modeling, and many more skills deemed necessary to survive. Leaders become leaders by building the capacity of the leadership organism in them through a relationship with the conglomerate of leadership skills. By performing these skills (or doing), we view the person as a leader. This brings us to what leaders ultimately do:

- Include others in the process to make informed decisions.

- Appreciate and recognize the merits of differing points of views.

- Seek out the counsel of mentors at the micro and macro level.

- Resolve their internal conflicts and help to resolve external conflicts using methods that promote trust, honor, and respect.

- Build sustainable and meaningful relationships self and others.

So far, we've discussed why we lead (to survive), what leadership is (a living, breathing organism), and what leadership does (take action from a conglomerate of skills used to influence change). The organism of leadership, inherent within all individuals, grows in the individual as they approach a need to survive, and respectively deploys the necessary act of leadership in order to ascertain their goal. Achieving their goals provides a sense of accomplishment that remains until the individual becomes challenged, seeing their current condition as stagnant, or has become bored. This may occur in areas of life, including physical, emotional, spiritual, financial, educational, or professional. As you see, leadership contains numerous layers and definitions. No matter what, the right leadership will facilitate your progress as the right person, in the right place, at the right time. It is toward this end that The Ellison Model serves as a rubric.

Reflective Journal Moment

3. Write about a time in your personal or professional life when you have felt stagnated. Write about the leadership role/position you took to survive and arrive to a sense of accomplishment.

Exercise: Maslow's Hierarchy of Needs

4. In which category do you see yourself in the Maslow Hierarchy of Needs?

5. List the steps you think you will have to take in order to arrive to the next level of need in your life.

THE ELLISON MODEL

Chapter 3

"You never change things by fighting the existing reality. To change something, build a new model that makes the existing model obsolete."

— R. Buckminster Fuller, American architect, systems theorist, author, designer, and inventor

Deryl G. Hunt, Ph.D. developed The Ellison Model (TEM) in 1994 as an intentional response to the increasing diversity in society and the world. The Ellison Model was also developed with a specific intent toward inclusive community building, quality management, and economic development that demonstrates inclusion, cultural sensitivity, and appreciation. Understanding the social conflicts plaguing our systems of humanity, including the individual and the global environment, The Ellison Model paradigm is a conceptual framework that focuses on relationship building with a holistic alternative method of delivering programs and services (Hunt, 2007). The holistic approach offered by Hunt (2007) involves a community of people acting in concert to perform organizational tasks. The Model suggests that all stakeholders benefit when people work harmoniously to create an inclusive environment.

The Model was named after Dr. Helen Ellison, who, at the time was Associate Vice President of Student Affairs at Florida International University. Dr. Hunt noted Dr. Ellison's skillful approach to establishing a harmonious environment of diverse individuals in the work place. The distinctive element of The Ellison Model is the inclusive community building approach, "a lens through which individuals can view themselves and the world around them" (www.icbproductions.net). Since its inception, The Model has grown in dimension and has been the subject of several books and dissertations.

As a multi-dimensional platform, The Ellison Model establishes accountability measures across all areas of life. It tests the relationship an individual has with themselves and others, as well as the relationships that institutions have with internal and external stakeholders. Most importantly, The Ellison Model shapes and reshapes attitudes toward inclusive community building. This is reflected in behaviors that care, share, and love; reinforced with affirming communication; and sustained through a disciplined demeanor. The Ellison Model is a praxis revolution to align individuals and their goals to the right approach and motivations. Revolution, for our purpose, like a wheel, means revolving or rotating back to the principles of inclusive community building.

The Ellison Model is comprised of several components, allowing for adaptability across industries and disciplines while maintaining consistent values. The following are essential components of The Ellison Model approach:

1. The Five Foci
2. The Vectors of (Potential) Conflict
3. The Inclusive Community-Discommunity Circular Diagram
4. The 7-Step Process for Character and Economic Development
5. Hunt's Theorem
6. The Ellison Model Principles Associative Graph
7. The Ellison Model Techniques
8. Keywords of The Ellison Model

The forthcoming chapters on The Model will also lay the framework for the Cole's Leadership-Solution Bridge, The Hunt Experiential Leadership Process (The HELP), and TEM Principles Associative Graph, three new concepts being presented for the first time.

THE ELLISON MODEL FIVE FOCI

Alicia Ritchey, Ed.D. is a curriculum expert, educator, and contributor to the body of work on The Ellison Model. Her expertise on The Model made her the ideal partner in editing this book. With both of us having been under the tutelage of Hunt, Ritchey and I have known each other for over two decades in which she has been both a mentor and partner in various projects including training and collaborating on initiatives involving The Model. Ritchey (2012) provides the following definitions on the five foci of the five major content areas that principally embody The Ellison Model: 1) inclusion, 2) multicultural appreciation, 3) mentorship, 4) conflict resolution, and 5) relationship building:

Foci #1 Inclusion: The traditional perspective of inclusion is the practice of incorporating the views and ideals of only those who are considered to be important. Inclusion in a traditional sense might only allow for the incorporation of those of like backgrounds, such as education level, income, religious views, or gender. The Ellison Model describes inclusion as the practice of bringing in the views, ideals, and contributions of everyone in the community or group in order to have a greater knowledge base. In this way, one's knowledge is expanded to include the knowledge of all those in the collective group. As part of The Ellison Model philosophy, it is believed that with inclusion, everyone has access to greater knowledge and resources, not from just a single source, but from the entire community.

Foci #2 Multicultural Appreciation: The traditional perspective of multicultural appreciation is the acknowledgement of cultural differences centered mostly on ethnicity, nationality, and race. The Ellison Model views multicultural appreciation as an acknowledgement of multiple perspectives and ways of knowing resulting from individuals' differences such as socioeconomic backgrounds, lived and historical experiences, age, gender, and religious and political beliefs. The Ellison Model helps individuals use individual differences as a point of connection in order to increase their potential to build better relationships with others. At this point, relationships are initiated and in time, the original differences that shaped individuals' perspectives–differences that once existed between individuals, groups, or communities--lose their significance. Now relationships continue to develop around an appreciation for similarities (grounded in The Ellison Model values of trust, honor, and respect) that are found in the process of relationship building in spite of the initial differences brought by the various parties.

Foci #3 Mentorship: The traditional perspective of mentorship is the practice of guidance and support by those who are empowered toward those in need; however, the mentor is typically the only person in the mentor-mentee relationship dispensing knowledge while the mentee/protégé is the only person in the relationship who is learning. The Ellison Model describes mentorship as the commitment of those with knowledge to share in the guidance and support to the least knowledgeable. The Ellison Model believes that everyone is a mentor and works to assist individuals in recognizing and embracing their capacity as mentors in order to strengthen their leadership capabilities. Within The Ellison Model framework, everyone is both mentor and mentee, simultaneously. In this case, while the mentor is dispensing knowledge, they are also receiving knowledge.

Foci #4 Conflict Resolution: The traditional perspective of conflict resolution is the management of outward behaviors between two separate parties. Conflict resolution within The Ellison Model framework requires that people first understand conflict as an internal turmoil/struggle, therefore a unitary process. The Ellison Model works with individuals to help them identify internal conflict in order to lead them through a process whereby the individual becomes unified internally and then progress towards unified relationships with others.

Foci #5 Relationship Building: The traditional perspective of relationship building is the process of individuals attempting to create bonds with other persons of interest – persons who may be of like-minds and who may share commonalities such as goals, interests, experiences, ancestries, and socio-economic backgrounds. The Ellison Model views relationships as the collective out of the integration of inclusion, effective mentorship, multicultural appreciation, and conflict resolution. Relationship building within The Ellison Model does not have to be pursued, but is an inevitable by-product when the other foci are in effect."

The five foci of The Ellison Model function in a unique way. While the whole is greater than the sum of its parts, it simultaneously maintains the wholeness of its sum in its parts. In other words, none of the parts can operate in isolation of the whole, even when focusing on it parts. Here's a personal example:

One afternoon, my father and I were peered with two other players for a round of golf. We had played with one of the gentlemen before. He was a very nice guy who was also a children's book author. Interestingly enough, his name was Arthur. He had brought his ten-year-old son along to play this time. The four of us, a two father-son pair, worked through the long nine-hole course at Greynolds Park in Miami, Florida. On hole four, Arthur's son made an incredible shot down the fairway. The ten-year-old could really swing the club. Personally, I was a novice at the game. I had some good swings and some good attempts. But overall, my game was in need of a lot of work. Notwithstanding, I enjoyed the game and at least understood the mechanics of playing. At one point during our round, the young player offered me advice.

"Nice shot," I said.

"Thank you," he replied.

I then approached my ball, swung, and watched it not be as nice as his shot.

He then asked, "Can I tell you something about your shot?"

"Sure young man," I replied with my eyes slightly squinted.

He proceeded to give me a pointer or two about my swing to which I replied, "Okay, cool. Thanks."

The entire interaction may have seemed innocent. But close examination of my mindset revealed to me that my attitude toward the ten-year-old needed to be re-aligned to the tenets of The Ellison Model. First, referring to him as "young man" was to draw a clear distinction between our differences in age. This was an effort to establish myself as his superior. It was intended to serve as a warning to him to be mindful in his communication because I was his elder. While his feedback may have been plausible, I had to determine whether I would accept his feedback or not. I was asking myself, "Should I be taking golf tips from a ten-year-old?"

The entirety of the five foci can be seen in each part of my interaction. I first needed to be inclusive to hear good feedback from anyone, including a ten-year-old who had more experience than I did in playing golf. Also, my initial reluctance was based on the conflict I allowed to manifest because of our age difference. I needed to resolve that conflict. His advice about my golf swing was a mentoring moment. Our age difference was not the measure by which to assess the interaction; it was his greater experience in the game of golf. If anything, I should have appreciated the difference in our age that albeit he was younger, he was still willing to help me improve my game as a fellow golfer. My reaction to his advice and throughout the rest of the round would ultimately have an impact on the quality of the relationship he and I would build. To ensure the proper alignment, I engaged him more throughout the fellow rounds and made sure to thank him for his earlier feedback. But this time, my "thank you" was from a genuine heart.

As you see, the five foci are always in play and to focus on any one of them in particular will always include the others. The parts contain the sum.

Moreover, take particular note that the implementation of the first four foci culminates into the fifth foci, relationship building. The relationships we build and sustain with others provide us the most important capital anyone can have: human capital, which puts great emphasis on who you know and not what you know. Who you know can give you access to what you need to know.

VECTORS OF PERSPECTIVES, DIVERSITY, AND (POTENTIAL) CONFLICT

Unfortunately, certain things get in the way of us building and sustaining effective relationships with people. The differing perspectives of individuals are used too often to create division as opposed to recognizing that people are more alike than they are different. Individuals use different things to draw a line in the sand to differentiate between themselves and others. According to The Ellison Model, some of the arbitrary metrics often used to draw differences between people may include: ethnicity, educational level, lived and historical experiences, religious persuasion, socio-economic status, language, age, and gender. The Ellison Model refers to such differences as the Vectors of Diversity, Vectors of Conflict, or Vectors of Perspectives & (Potential) Conflict (Ritchey, 1999; Rice, 2001; Hunt, 2003).

Ethnicity	Education Level	Lived & Historical Experiences
Religious Persuasion	**PERSPECTIVES**	Socio-Economic Status
Language	Age	Gender

Fig. 2

At one juncture, the diversity between people is to be celebrated. However, those same points of diversity can become the same source of conflict. As seen in my recount of the ten-year-old golfer, age was used as a means to (internal) conflict. We witness these vectors of diversity leapfrogging into conflict on a daily basis in our own inter-personal experiences, and even as far as conflict between nations.

Ethnicity: conflict arises on the basis of an individual's culture, race, nationality, language, or ancestry. Individuals or groups of people are convinced to see themselves as superior or inferior to others based on the categorization imposed upon them. The value system they create subjectively informs them of what is right from wrong or acceptable from unacceptable. The conflict works top-down and bottom-up. The dominant group may see others as below them and resort to oppressive actions. The minority group may develop resentment toward those who consider themselves as part of the majority.

Education level: conflict arises on the value we give to our level of education. This is usually in the context of formal education and professional experience. A person with a lower level of formal education might be conflicted in thinking that those with a higher degree are highfalutin. In contrast, those with a higher degree might consider those with a lower degree as subordinate, less dignified or less knowledgeable. Education level can also be reflective of socio-economic differences amongst individuals. Typically, those with higher levels of education are more likely to earn higher wages, which transfers into better living conditions and access to more affluent neighborhoods. The conflict arises in the exclusion and lack of appreciation of multiple perspectives based on an individual's educational level. Conflict on the basis of educational level also reflects a combination of other potential conflicts including ethnicity, socio-economics, and classism.

Lived and historical experiences: conflict arises from the social identity individuals have developed based on knowledge acquired through their lived and historical experiences. Having first-hand experiences makes the individual more prone to "know what they know" and create firm conclusions about approaches to life. Their conclusions establish a methodology for leading and resolving conflict in a way that presents stability and progress within group settings and their personal lives. Conflict arises in at least two ways as a result of the conclusions individuals adopt. First, the individual practices exclusion and lack of appreciation of the lived and historical experiences of others. When this happens, there is a tendency for the individual to see others as lacking experience because they have not shared the same experiences. Secondly, others practice exclusion and lack of appreciation by denouncing the lived and historical experiences of "seasoned professionals" by seeing them as lacking creativity, being rigid, or stuck in antiquated ways of doing things. The conflict appears to center on a showdown between experience versus creativity (or what some may see as risk taking). Sentiments of "this is how we've always done it" come into play as individuals struggle to maintain the status quo while others challenge it (based on the experiences of or lack thereof of both parties). In other words, the lived and historical experiences of individuals help to shape their point of view into conservative, moderate, or liberal leadership.

Socio-economic status: conflict arises from the value individuals place on their education, income, and occupation. Education, income, and occupation invariably impacts an individuals access to upward mobility, sphere of influence, and material possessions including houses, automobiles, and clothing. This often draws a distinct line between the haves and the have-nots. Education, income, and occupation are often used to measure worldly success. The two-way perception that both the haves and the have-nots have toward each other based on a person's station in life can be a catalyst to conflict. People who have acquired a certain socio-economic success may reject and treat poorly those who have not acquired the same level of affluence. Conversely, those who are less affluent may resent, judge, and think poorly of the more affluent. As you see, conflict is not top-down or bottom-up, but cyclical as relationships evolve and devolve. Conflict arises in the exclusion and lack of appreciation of diverse perspectives based on an individual's socio-economic status.

Age, language, religious persuasion, and gender all follow the same formula of conflict: exclusion and lack of appreciation of the perspectives of others based on a line of thinking that either undermines or overstates the value of an individual, group, or community. In addition to the original seven categories of the Vectors of Conflict, other perspectives can also serve as points of potential conflict at which individuals intersect. The perspectives include occupation, communication style, conflict resolution style, personality trait, physical and mental health, political affiliation and viewpoints, nationality, entertainment lifestyle, family name, marital status, parental status and sexual orientation. I added these additional perspectives to the list in order to more holistically consider the multiple forums in which people develop perspectives through their ongoing lived and historical experiences. As you have no doubt observed, individuals are capable of using a wide array of contingencies to promulgate conflict.

Furthermore, the perspectives, while lengthy, can be neatly categorized under one of the following five headings: Economic, Psychological, Political, Religious, or Social. Journals and books throughout business management, political sciences, religious studies, psychology, and the social sciences consistently note how each of these areas impact one another and are not independent of one another (Marx, 1844; De Saussure, 1906-1911; Forgette, Dettrey, Boening, Van Swanson, 2011; Robinson, 2015; Lemert, 2017). Ultimately, you cannot understand the social world around you without understanding how the economic, psychological, political, and religious sectors work in tandem throughout every society.

Similar to how the sum of the five foci operates within its parts, It is safe to say that an individual's perspectives do not work in isolation of one another in their potential to generate conflict. An individual who demonstrates exclusion or a lack of appreciation of others on the basis of any criteria may develop a certain style or approach toward others they exclude, setting the foundation for other perspectives to be used as a vector of conflict. It is a snowball effect that may begin with any perspective found in Figure 3 and end with many more perspectives added over time. For example, an individual may have social status based on their family name, in which they practice exclusion and lack of appreciation of others outside of their family. Next, they use the notoriety of their family name as a segue to amass political power. With that political power they are able to stack the economic cards in their favor, thereby infringing on other groups. The individual's communication style to others outside of their family, political, and religious affluence may be demeaning and condescending. We can go on and on compounding the vectors of conflict. This example obviously paints a very conflicted person, but toward the end of demonstrating how perspectives do not work in isolation. Figure 3 outlines the updated vectors of perspectives, diversity, and potential conflict with the corresponding categories.

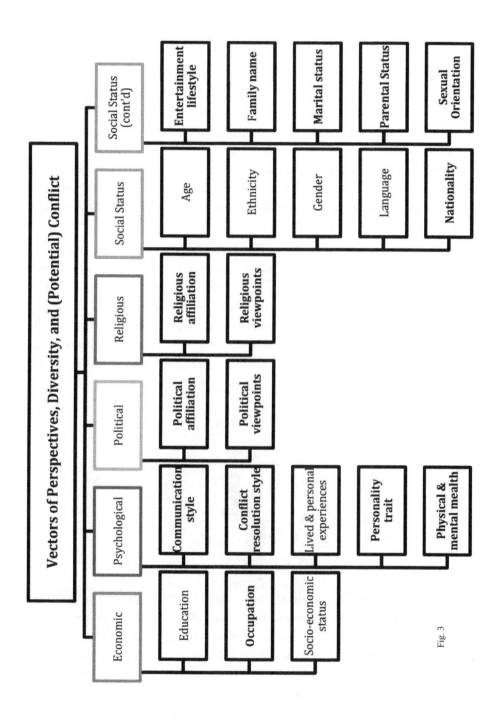

Vectors of Perspectives, Diversity, and (Potential) Conflict

Economic
- Education
- Occupation
- Socio-economic status

Psychological
- Communication style
- Conflict resolution style
- Lived & personal experiences
- Personality trait
- Physical & mental mealth

Political
- Political affiliation
- Political viewpoints

Religious
- Religious affiliation
- Religious viewpoints

Social Status
- Age
- Ethnicity
- Gender
- Language
- Nationality

Social Status (cont'd)
- Entertainment lifestyle
- Family name
- Marital status
- Parental Status
- Sexual Orientation

Fig. 3

for the emerging leader

Spaces, Environment, and Relationships

People everywhere and anywhere occupy physical spaces at specific times in a specific role. For example, from 6 a.m. to 7:30 a.m. Tiffany occupies her two-bedroom condo as mother of a two-year-old daughter. She prepares and drops her daughter to school every morning by 8:15 a.m. Then from 9 a.m. to 5 p.m. Tiffany occupies the corner office of a law firm in which she was recently named a partner. Tiffany tutors once a week in a program associated with her daughter's elementary school. When the weekend arrives, Tiffany can be found in the art and design district of Wynwood eating, dancing, and laughing away with her group of friends.

Tiffany occupies the spaces of her condo, law office, the homes of her friends and family, her daughter's elementary school, and the city's entertainment locations. She also occupies the roads and other services found throughout the city such as gas stations, grocery stores, malls, and banks. She can be found in these spaces at very specific times determined by how she coordinates her schedule. The spaces she occupies at the time she occupies them are done so in the role of mother, employee, friend, patron, and resident.

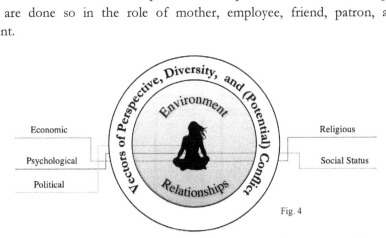

Fig. 4

The conglomerate of these spaces, times, and roles creates Tiffany's environment. The environment, the social and cultural demographics of Tiffany's life, simultaneously impacts her as she impacts it. In this exchange, Tiffany has established a relationship with the environment. However, the environment is only symbolic of its creators: people, animals, or nature. In a metropolitan city, for the sake of this scenario, her relationship is reflected through her interaction with the people who comprises the environment. Subsequently, her environment is defined by the relationships she has with the people in each of the spaces she occupies. Essentially, Tiffany's relationships constitute her sphere of influence. And as all individuals do, Tiffany brings all of who she is, reflected through her various perspectives, into each space she visits, the overall environment, and most importantly, to each relationship she has forged.

How Tiffany chooses to engage others with her perspectives and respond to the perspectives of others sets the stage for conflict and conflict resolution. Conflict is not always negative. Sometimes referred to as constructive conflict (Hocker & Wilmot, 2014; Ramsbotham, Woodhouse, & Miall, 2011), the collision of perspectives can be used as a learning opportunity for all parties involved. An individual's attitude toward the conflict makes the strongest case as to whether the conflict will be constructive or destructive.

Individuals and groups usually operate from the sum total of their multiple perspectives on any given subject matter. Rice & Rice (2013) refers to points of perspectives as the Social Constructions of Culture. The construction of culture occurs through the culmination of multiple perspectives developed through multiple forums over time. Tiffany, for example, in her relationships, operates as a female with very distinct experiences accumulated through her gender, socio-economic status, income level, and educational level in addition to her previous experiences. All of these factors impact how she practices law, raises her child, and interacts with others in the community. As such, you can think of perspectives as a response to the accumulation of an individual's time, space, and environment. In other words, Tiffany's socialized response is her typical answer to any given question. Her answer is not the only answer or her absolute answer in all situations – It is simply her perspective at that time. Understanding Tiffany's background helps us understand her thought process and decision-making process.

All suggested answers, including the ones that appear to lack substance, could add something new, profound, or creative to the process. The Ellison Model approach asserts that the right answer is found in the inclusiveness of the process that allows room for diverse answers to be presented without discredit. By creating and promoting a space for sharing, you encourage the growth and development of others and steadily push them toward a partnership in the inclusive community building process. Open-mindedness to various perspectives can also show you where your counterparts, subordinates, or supervisors are in their thinking and understanding on any given issue. It benefits everyone to demonstrate multi-cultural appreciation of diverse perspectives.

THE ELLISON MODEL
COMMUNITY-DISCOMMUNITY CIRCULAR DIAGRAM

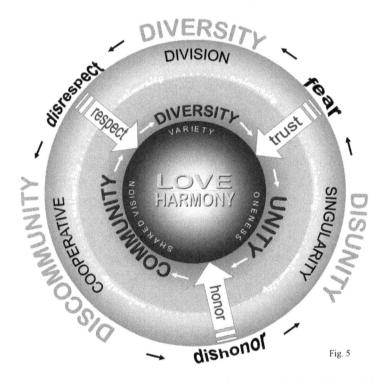

Fig. 5

The Community-Discommunity Circular Diagram of The Ellison Model is comprised of the inner-circle and the outer-circle. In the inner-circle, you will find a character development process with several components of clockwise movement including: from diversity, to unity, to community and from variety, to oneness, to a shared vision. At the center of the inner-circle is the motivating factor of love or harmony. Movement into the inner-circle requires an individual's transition from the discommunity values found in the counterclockwise movement of the outer-circle. Movement in the outer-circle is regressive as it moves individuals from diversity, to discommunity, to disunity, fueled by intentions of division (as in being divisive), cooperatives, and singularities. Transition from the outer-circle to the inner-circle requires the transforming and transcendence of disrespect to respect, dishonor to honor, and fear to trust amongst individuals and groups. Animosity is found as the fueling agent at the core of this counter-clockwise, regressive movement.

The Community-Discommunity Circular Diagram examines an individual's motivation while seeking to realign their mindset toward inclusive community building. Inclusive community building occurs when the holistic community of stakeholders within an organization or group commits itself to quality management and economic development that demonstrates inclusion, cultural sensitivity, and appreciation. Inclusive community building does not fall short of considering and protecting the environment, employees, shareholders, and the greater society. It is the awareness that every action taken by the individual, group, or organization has an immediate or long-term impact on society. It is also the willingness to hold one's self personally and corporately responsible for the imprints we leave on society. In a family setting, the requirements remain the same. Family members, the same as stakeholders, whether immediate or extended, are considered a part of the community. However, no one, whether family, corporate, municipal, or otherwise, can be considered a part of the inclusive community until he or she is willing to be included. This makes the inclusive community building process a unitary process for all leaders to immerse themselves.

Discommunity vs. Inclusive Community Building

The Community-Discommunity Circular Diagram of The Ellison Model encourages leaders to move from the counterclockwise or counterproductive outer-circle of discommunity building, in which leaders lead by disrespect, fear, dishonesty, and competitiveness. Instead leaders are encouraged to refocus their leadership approach to a clockwise or progressive inner-circle that is energized by trust, honor, and respect. It is easy to confuse an exclusive community or discommunity for an inclusive community in a group setting as the group works toward a common goal. Discommunities are formed as factions and cliques that seek to operate out of competitiveness for the individual and group interests at the expense of anyone not considered a part of the group. Take the housing market for instance, and the crash of 2008 wherein bankers, brokers, and real estate agents worked on their personal behalf to inflate prices in the housing market. Many capitalized through credit default swaps and the intentional shorting of collateralized mortgage obligations. While the group of bankers, brokers, and real estate agents worked together to buttress their income, they actually worked as an exclusive community or discommunity in which they held their personal interest in front of the greater societal interest.

Sociologist Claire Michele Rice, Ph. D. (2001) describes discommunity as follows: "the community in a state of discommunity is much more of a cooperative, whose goal is to advance only the social and economic welfare of those belonging to the group. They may share the same race, ancestry or belief system. Ultimately, animosity/hate is the central value esteemed by discommunity builders while that esteemed by true community builders is harmony/love." Subsequently, leaders must love the people and the community they serve and make decisions that build the inclusive community of our overall society. "The term *community building* describes efforts to shape and mold the social [economical, personal, political, and religious] environment(s) in which people live" toward the intrinsic values of The Ellison Model's inner-circle, which is harmony/love (Hunt & Hunt, 2008).

Buy-in into any area of the Vectors of (Potential) Conflict places the individual on the outer-circle of the Community-Discommunity Circular Diagram. When individuals are conflicted internally, and they come together in a group setting, the inevitable outcome is more conflict. Conflict may not only occur between members of the group, but decisions that are made out of a state of conflict will ostracize others who are not in the personal interest of the group members. For example, in the corporate setting of higher education, staff members from multiple student affairs and academic affairs' departments meet to coordinate the commencement ceremony. Where department representatives are operating on the fringe of discommunity building, you will find them safeguarding and insulating themselves from responsibilities toward the event planning process. They may inform everyone of how busy their staff already are, undermine ideas, attempt to cut the meeting short, show very little enthusiasm for the event, arrive late or not attend the meeting at all, just to name a few scenarios. Representatives may try to put the work off on another department; or depending on the influence of group think, may decide to overlook some things that is in the best interest of the graduates. These kinds of meetings are often unproductive. Leaders who share at heart the best interest of the inclusive community may easily see the shortcomings of the committee and request they meet again with an updated itinerary.

Because conflict resolution is a unitary process, and conflict places an individual on the outer-circle, the process to move from the outer-circle to the inner-circle is also a unitary process. While aided by a mentor, the decision is ultimately up to the individual to accept the change. As individuals move from the outer-circle into the inner-circle, they are able to move others from diversity to unity to inclusive community building wherein diversity is seen as a starting point and not the end goal of community building. "Diversity, if motivated by animosity/hate, yields a negative value of disrespect. As the relationship develops under this value system, it leads to discommunity" (Hunt & Hunt, 2008).

Diversity

The Ellison Model takes an evolved position on the matter of diversity by seeing diversity as a starting point in the community building process. While many leaders embrace diversity as a celebration of our differences, The Ellison Model notes that the same differences we celebrate are the same differences we use to separate us. For example, in a friendship between two young girls, one girl wore glasses. The friend was complimentary of her friend's eyewear, often commenting on how smart and interesting it made her look. When the two had a falling out, the same friend made fun of the girl with glasses by calling her four-eyes and Blind Batty. The same diversity that was celebrated in her eyewear was the same diversity used against the friend with glasses. While diversity is often celebrated in our societies, upon close inspection, diversity often creates as much of a rift between individuals and groups despite our attempt to make it seem as an embraceable attribute. The truth is that we function and operate more cohesively because human beings, across all nations and cultures, have more in common than not. Furthermore, the suffix 'di' means two. The circular diagram offers progress from twoness to oneness, which is found in unity. The transition from diversity to unity is an emphasis on the qualities that make us alike stressing oneness. From there, we move onto to community, where a shared vision of communal responsibility is a necessary step in the inclusive community building process. Otherwise, we inadvertently create discommunities.

Motive for Relationship Building

The circular diagram outlines the motivations of individuals and the resulting outcome. Throughout the diagram, an individual may be motivated to build community, thus moving in a clockwise rotation propelled by trust, honor, and respect. Contrarily, one may build discommunity, hence a counter-clockwise rotation in motions of fear, dishonor, and disrespect. If the five foci are always in use, culminating into how we build relationships, then the circular diagram serves as the internal compass that reveals an individual's motivation for building relationships. As stated, individuals are motivated to build relationships through either attitudes of inclusive community-building or discommunity building. In other words, they are building relationships that commit to the communal good; otherwise they build for their personal gain to the detriment of the community.

Building relationships according to The Ellison Model requires leaders to operate in the clockwise position of the circular diagram. Otherwise, to operate in the counter-clockwise rotation make certain consequences imminent, including cliques and unity amongst subsets of the community for the purpose of forwarding the personal mission of specific individuals. We see this time and time again in business, politics, faith-based organizations, education, and individuals. The capitalistic practice of many corporate entities is to use competition in order to drive innovation and fast track production. Sometimes called "healthy competition", it still provides a breeding ground for dis-community building because individuals are forced to focus on their personal success in order to remain relevant to the company. I contend, however, that the same gains in innovation and productivity can be achieved through the efforts of inclusion far more than the efforts of competition. In the inherent desire to survive, progress, and have a sense of accomplishment, human beings come pre-packaged with the necessary level of desire to compete and drive innovation. The circular diagram maps an approach to help leaders steer this innate drive within individuals from diversity, to unity, to inclusive community building.

GOMABCD: 7-STEP PROCESS OF CHARACTER DEVELOPMENT & COMMUNITY BUILDING

The 7-Step Process of Character Development and Community Building (Hunt, 2006a) is a pragmatic approach to character education, economic development, and community affairs for social development. The 7-Step process uses a two-part approach, as reflected in GOMA and ABCD, for a variety of training across education, government, business, and faith-based organizations. Among the essential uses of the 7-Step process are: 1) a strategic planning tool; 2) a mapping and analysis tool; 3) a non-descript entity for character education; 4) a faith-based tool for developing church leaders; 5) and a visual guide for self-reflection and personal development. As shown in the image (Figure 6), GOMABCD teaches individuals how to make the right

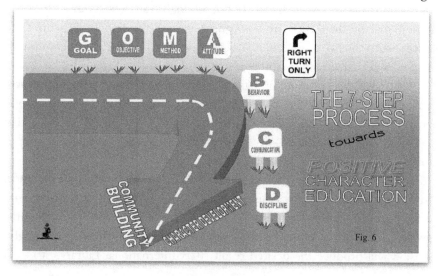

Fig. 6

for the emerging leader

turn toward community building and character and economic development.

GOMA is an acronym for Goal, Objective, Method, and Attitude. Each letter is linked to a certain characteristic intended to reflect a specific intrinsic value. G stands for goal. The goal is Community. GOMA grounds the individual or group's goal toward inclusive community building. O stands for objective. The objective is Unity. GOMA sets objectives that unify. M stands for method. The method is Respect. GOMA employs methods that respect "the rights and ways of others." Lastly, A stands for attitude. The attitude is Honor. GOMA maintains an attitude of honor toward one another and the community at-large (Hunt, 2006a).

ABCD, the second part of the 7-Step Process, is also an acronym for Attitude, Behavior, Communication, and Discipline (Hunt, 2006a). ABCD ensures that the implementation of the goals, objectives, methods, and attitude, the accompanying disposition of heart, are reflective of an "inclusive community building attitude that contains caring, sharing, and loving behaviors, in addition to affirming communication that yield discipline or the sustainability of a desired outcome" (Hunt, 2008; Ritchey, 2012, p. 146). Put together, this creates the GOMABCD 7-Step Process. Similar to the circular diagram, GOMABCD also points to the internal decision-making process each individual undergoes when confronted with daily issues. While the circular diagram focuses on movement in the progressive, clockwise position, the GOMABCD 7-Step Process indicates that doing the right thing is a matter of making the right turn. The right turn is a decision that reinforces character. However, note that a continuous right turn results in a clockwise motion, making the 7-Step process consistent with the circular diagram. Both conceptual frameworks within The Model reinforce inclusive community building and character development.

There are three important aspects of the 7-Step Process to note. First, some models reflect the ABC's of their particular processes. However, the D for discipline sets The Ellison Model apart as the critical element that highlights the importance of continuously making the right turn or continuously striving to do the right thing.

Second, GOMA and the ABCD's connect at the juncture of Attitude. Attitude guides the process from the goal to the implementation phase onto to the outcomes. "Look at the process as a traveler on a journey. When the traveler comes to a crossroads, the right [attitude followed by the right] decision will produce the desired result (ICB International Library, 2014). A leader's attitude is the pivotal turning point in providing and maintaining leadership as prescribed by the tenets of The Ellison Model. In the Inclusive Community-Discommunity Circular Diagram, an individual's attitude can be seen as the catalyst that drives the process clockwise toward community building or counterclockwise toward discommunity building. Going back to an earlier example, I made the *right turn* in my **attitude;** subsequently, it reflected in my **behavior** and **communication** to the ten-year-old golfer who served as my *mentor* during that round of golf. Third, the 7-Step process works to simultaneously align external approaches with internal motivations.

Strategic Planning & Program Development

GOMABCD is also an organizational tool for strategic planning and program development. The 7-Step Process has been widely used across the U.S and abroad. In 2006, the Turks and Caicos Social Services Department reached out for community development training for their government officials and local residents to assist with poverty alleviation in the country. Using the 7-Step Process, , I, along with a team of other Ellison Model trainers, worked under the leadership of Dr. Hunt to create and conduct training on a project called the Poverty Alleviation & Citizen Empowerment (PACE) Initiative. In 2007, the Island Special Constabulary Force in Westmoreland, Jamaica requested and received training for their police officers on Community Building & Urban Renewal Training using the 7-Step Process. In 2008, the 7-Step Process was used in Freeport, Grand Bahamas to train residents and government officials from the Social Services Department on urban renewal in a project called The ABCD's of Character Development and Urban Renewal.

The 7-Step Process has also been used to steer the curriculum of leadership and character development programs. One such program was the Operation BICOH Cordele Youth Summer Institute, hosted in Cordele, Georgia from 2007 to present. Similarly, the 7-Step Process has been used for program development at colleges and universities throughout the nation for both student and staff development for over a decade. As you see, the components of The Ellison Model are real world tools that impact leaders and their ability to strategically plan.

As mentioned before, the programmatic approach of the 7-Step process works to simultaneously align external approaches with internal motivations. G-O-M-A outlines the goal, objectives, method, and attitude of an individual or groups' approach toward any given project. Concurrently, GOMA advocates that the goal is community building, the objective is to unify, the method is respect, and the attitude is to honor. In this instance, GOMA plays a dual role:

1. GOMA outlines the tangible goals, objectives, method, and attitude of the project; and

2. GOMA links the intrinsic values necessary for building community, unity, respect, and honor between project coordinators and stakeholders.

In this approach, GOMA aim to align the project coordinators' or event planners' actions to the intent of their purpose. The right intention helps to uphold the spirit and act of good will by maintaining the focus on the tenets of community building. While serving as the director of student life and leadership development at Broward College, I worked with our programming board students to coordinate a campus and community wide health fair. The student leaders and I met with the nursing department chair and faculty members to initiate the planning and execution. The event involved several heath service vendors throughout Broward County, including the Broward County Health Department. The following is a practical example of how the 7-Step process might be used to strategically coordinate an upcoming event such as a health fair:

Community Health Fair Event

Goal: build an inclusive community by raising awareness of the benefits of a healthy lifestyle.

Objective: foster unity by

- Providing free health screenings, information and demonstrations;

- Providing positive health behavior changes;

- Increasing awareness of local, state, and national health services and resources.

Method: promote respect of self and others by providing the following services (at no cost):

- Blood type testing
- HIV testing
- Blood pressure testing
- Glucose testing
- Pamphlets on various health topics
- Directory of health websites and 1-800 numbers

Attitude: promote an honorable obligation to successfully execute the project.

The Ellison Model sees the **goal** of any task as a community building effort, no matter the nature and scope of the project. Whether picking up an empty can from the ground and putting it in the garbage to drafting legislation for the country, every act we take impacts our larger society. Every action sets an example and creates precedence for another individual or group to use as a foundation.

The target audience of the event is not to be confused with the inclusive community-building goal. The target audience is the specific group for whom the event will set the foundation. In the example of the health fair, the event can be hosted by the Department of Health for the entire county or hosted by the human resources department for all employees of that specific company. In either case, the participants, citizens of earth, learn the importance of community building through healthy lifestyle. The education and awareness to one individual at the health fair can create a far-reaching ripple effect on many more people within an individuals' sphere of influence, including their friends and family.

The intrinsic **objective** of the health fair planning committee is to foster unity. Unity is created through the buy-in evident by the community's participation as people are brought together for a common cause on which they can all agree, in this case, health awareness. The tangible objective speaks to the things the planning committee aims to do in order to accomplish the goal.

The intrinsic **method** promotes respect for self and others in the actual work required to acquire the services for the event. In making phone calls, sending emails, and making requests of different agencies, in other words, when engaging stakeholders, the program coordinators must respectfully engage. The tangible methods are the actual products in hand for the end-users.

The intrinsic **attitude** of honor serves to ensure the success and excellence of the initiative. In the planning and execution of the event, we honor life and a healthy lifestyle for everyone; we honor the underserved by serving them; and, we honor those unaware by educating them. In the case of the health fair community event, the tangible attitude is expressed by honoring the health professionals with a platform to provide their services.

An individual's attitude is the most crucial element of community building. Subsequently, the A for attitude is reflected in both GOMA and ABCD. The attitude is where we make the right or wrong turn in our disposition of heart; It is where we decide to embrace or reject the goal, objective, and method. Consequently, Attitude guides our behavior, communication, and how we demonstrate discipline toward self and others in the community. Furthermore, it shapes and drives the quality of an individual or group's motivation. The A-B-C-D reflects the demonstrative values in outward actions when interacting with others. Specifically, behavior and communication indicate the level of professionalism reflected in how we pursue and build relationships. That may include how we speak to others in conversation, how we dress for an occasion, and how we conduct ourselves within a particular space. The D for discipline is our ability to consistently approach all matters with the right attitude, behavior, and communication.

Goma Goes to School

GOMA, in addition to being an acronym, has also been used as the name of a non-descript character in a series of books written by Hunt (2006a) and a team of curriculum writers. The series of books present Goma as a young boy who "experiences moral and ethical dilemmas" amongst his neighbors, friends, and classmates. We get to see Goma grow up and mature to experience issues of love and marriage, work life, and other experiences as he matures into a character-filled individual who demonstrates the right attitude, behavior, communication, and discipline. Teachers in the classroom as well as summer programs that teach character education have used these series of books.

"Let us introduce you to Goma. Goma is a good student who has goals to succeed in life, and he tries to find ways of achieving them. Just as everyone, he is constantly faced with important decisions, but he is open to learning ways to make right choices. Think about your own goals and aspirations. Think of the questions above as you learn about Goma, his values and how his experiences are helpful in shaping his character." (Excerpt from Meet Goma, The ICB Character Education & Community Building Book Series)

As The Ellison Model has evolved over the past two decades, Goma has become the signature component used to teach and demonstrate the model's effectiveness. Another educational framework resulting from Goma is an initiative called The Kidz 4 Kidz Program, a character and entrepreneurial program for grade-level children and young adults. In all Goma led initiatives, Goma personifies and personalizes the process of inclusive-community building. The end game of Goma leads to the recognition that both you and I are Goma. Most people, if not all people, can identify with setting goals and objectives, and maintaining certain methods and attitudes toward its pursuit. Being the right person in the right place at the right time is found in the cornerstone of the 7-Step Process: Attitude. Moving from the outer-circle to the inner-circle of the circular diagram for inclusive community building is also found in having and demonstrating the right attitude.

HUNT'S THEOREM:
GIVEN ICBA, THEN CSLB + AC = D

Adopted by Ritchey (2012), Hunt's Theorem (Hunt, 2006a) is a cumulative formula that seamlessly brings together the multiple components of The Ellison Model to show how they interplay:

Hunt's Theorem offers profundity to questions related to community building within broad contexts. It states: "Given ICBA, then CSLB + AC = D," and is understood to mean: 'given an Inclusive Community Building Attitude, then Caring, Sharing, Loving Behaviors, as well as Affirming Communication yield Discipline or the sustainability of a desired outcome which is achieved through nurturing over time.' The desired outcome is that of an inclusive community, where elements of inclusion, multicultural appreciation, conflict resolution, mentoring, and relationship building are both inherent and conspicuous.

Hunt's Theorem further demonstrates how each component carries the wholeness of its parts. Lapse in any part of the formula easily causes a ripple effect throughout the process. The role of the mentor is that much more pivotal in order to safeguard against any such lapse in the leadership development process. Lapses can be best prevented or properly managed when all stakeholders see themselves as capable mentors no matter where they land in the vector of perspective (age, ethnicity, socio-economic status, or religion). In other words, no matter where you see yourself on the totem pole (if one even really exists) you are a mentor. Ultimately, the reliance on the strength of the group, including all stakeholders, is critical in the individual and group process of community building.

PRINCIPLES ASSOCIATIVE GRAPH

The foundational principles or meta-values of The Ellison Model are: trust, honor, respect, caring, sharing, and loving. The Five Foci, Community-Discommunity Circular Diagram, GOMAABCD 7-Step Process, and Hunt's Theorem among other components, consistently reveal these principles. The principles work together, as does The Model and its components, to address an individual's or group's motivation, attitude, and behavior toward self and others.

The Associative Graph illustrates the association between the six principles on a vertical and horizontal plane. Trust, honor, and respect aligns the attitude necessary to demonstrate caring, sharing, and loving behaviors in the process of moving one's self and others from diversity, to unity, to community. The vertical plane of trust, honor, and respect is reflective of an individual's inner-development of self, purpose, and a system of meta-values that transitions their disposition of heart from dis-community building to inclusive community building. This again speaks to the intrinsic values presented in the 7-Step Process, and can only be achieved by re-shifting thoughts into alignment of the *right attitude*. In their book *Encouraging Authenticity and Spirituality in Higher Education,* Chickering, Dalton, and Stamm (2006) discuss the impact of focusing on our vertical relationship. Higher education research professors and scholars Alexander W. Astin and Helen S. Astin stated the following inn the foreword of the book:

> Although American higher education can justifiably take pride in its capacity to develop the student's ability to manipulate the material world through its programs in science, medicine, technology, and commerce, it has paid relatively little attention to the student's "inner" development-- the sphere of values and beliefs, emotional maturity, moral development, spirituality, and self-understanding. What is most ironic about this neglect of the student's interior is that many of the great literary and philosophical traditions that constitute the core of a liberal education are grounded in the maxim, "know thyself." This imbalance in emphasis on outer versus inner development has enormous implications for the future not only of our society but also of the world. Self-understanding is fundamental to our capacity to understand others.

Coming into understanding of who you are and what you stand for may be 99% of the leadership development process. The Seven Vectors of Identity Development created by Arthur Chickering (1969), and later revisited by Chickering and Linda Reisser (1993), further complements the vertical plane by identifying aspects of identity development that must be internally reconciled by the individual. Those aspects include "managing emotions, moving through autonomy toward interdependence, establishing identity, developing purpose, and developing integrity." The inner-development is a vertical relationship that shapes a leader's attitude in developing a relationship with self.

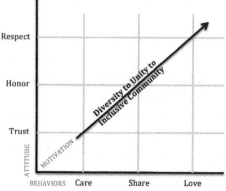

Fig. 7a

for the emerging leader

The horizontal plane of Care, Share, and Love is an external display of *the right behaviors* toward one's self and others that can only be realized as the internal process of trust, honor, and respect develops. In being an inclusive community builder, leaders must manage and legislate in ways that evidence care about the collective, share resources appropriately, and love through kindness, service, and the desire to see all people progress. In other words, the quality of one's inward development of his or her positive attitude that reflects Trust, Honor, and Respect is directly proportional to Caring, Sharing, and Loving behaviors, in which case, we progress in the development of our social, economical, and political societies, moving from diversity, to unity, to an inclusive community at an exponential rate of growth.

Trust. Trust is an essential part of the relational process (Levinger, 1979; Lewicki & Bunker, 1995; Scandura & Pellegrini, 2003), a vital principle to building genuine, long-term relationships. Merriam-Webster defines trust as "assured reliance on the character, ability, strength, or truth of someone or something; one in which confidence is placed." While leaders are encouraged to exhibit *Trust* by following the chain of command, trust the intentions of decision-makers, and trust the environment to nurture their development, some individual's in leadership roles, counterparts, and subordinates may be motivated to build dis-community and, in effect, break the trust you exhibit to them. Subsequently, the only guarantee in *Trust* is to trust the effectiveness of the principles of trust, honor, respect, caring, sharing, and loving with the most important sustainable outcome being your positive character and integrity as a leader. Where trust may be broken with individuals or the environment, maintaining Trust in the development process as a personal value equips leaders with a problem-solving record of achievement despite the obstacles they may face in the relationship building process.

Honor and Respect for Others. Traditionally speaking, honor and respect are often used interchangeably; however, The Ellison Model defines these two principles separately. Honor is a principle of character. In order for one to be honored, he or she must exude the necessary character that commands such honor. We might say that there is a direct correlation between the honor one deserves and the method by which one seeks it, whether through legitimate or illegitimate means. "Honor is reserved for the honorable" (Hunt, 2000a).

"To build the inclusive community, one must have Respect unto all **right ways**. Respect unto all right ways is the recognition that some ways are proper for civility and some are not" (Hunt, 2000a). Moreover, respect is a principle of character, in which the focus is placed on the right ways of operation, not the personality of individuals. Individuals sometimes overlook the contribution of others because they dislike the personality of the contributor. The Ellison Model recognizes, through its focus on inclusion, the honorable work brought to the table by all stakeholders while maintaining respect for the right ways of all.

Honor can be seen as a matter of scope. The President of the United States of America (POTUS), who expectedly honorably executes the function of office, receives more honor than the street sweeper who honorably sweeps the street. This is so because POTUS has a broader scope of responsibility with commensurate accountability than does the street sweeper. At the same time, poor execution by POTUS potentially has a farther-reaching impact than poor execution by the street sweeper. Relatively speaking, both POTUS and the street sweeper receive equal respect in their bid to execute their roles the right way. On the other hand, the honor given to POTUS is distinguishable from the street sweeper through their scope of responsibility and accountability.

You can understand how Honor and Respect work metaphorically by understanding the makeup of the United States Congress. Congress is comprised of two chambers: The Senate and The House of Representatives. States are allocated seats in The House of Representatives based on the number of residents in the State. The population size indicates the amount of resources needed to manage the State. Larger populations equal a greater scope in responsibility and accountability for State political officers including governors, senators, and representatives. Honor is similar to The House of Representatives in that honor is distributed according to the scope of responsibility and accountability. Conversely, no matter the State's population, each State has two Senate seats. The Senate does not look at size (breadth of scope), but equality for all States. Respect is similar to The Senate in that all people should be respected for their right ways no matter how 'big' their position.

Honor and Respect for Self. As leaders trust the process, they also Honor the process by embracing their own authenticity. You grow in authenticity as you discover your sense of self, purpose, and meta-values. Your authenticity is a genuine reflection of who you are in a way that is socially responsible and inclusive (Chickering, Dalton, Stamm, 2006; Hunt, 2006a). Too often we associate a monetary value to our worth. In effect, we lower our value by tying it to money. Being true to yourself will help guide you to your purpose. But your purpose in life may not come with a big monetary payoff. The best things in life really are free. The Ellison Model offers you those things freely: caring, sharing, loving, trust, respect, and honor. These values may lead you to work as a caretaker in a poverty-stricken country in which you have no luxury of sorts other than the air you breath. Conditions may be hot and humid. The food may be scarce. But your contribution would be immeasurable. Consider the lives you can touch, the families you can save, and the love you can show. No one can pay you any amount of money to be true to yourself. Still when your true self shows up, my, oh my, what an amazingly, gifted and impactful leader you will be!

Leadership Positions vs. Being Positioned to Lead

Leadership is not about positions. This is probably the biggest misnomer made by emerging leaders. They assume you must hold a certain title in order to affect change. Change happens through influence, not titles. Influence comes from the honor and respect you have garnered within the community. Ultimately, this is exactly what The Ellison Model does: provide you the means to most effectively and genuinely garner the power of influence through inclusive community building strategies. You will observe this truth over time. People in general have a way of knowing when someone is being genuine and transparent in their dealings. Your leadership approach will indicate over time whether you are an inclusive community builder or discommunity builder. The world needs honest leaders who honor and respect their constituents, not leaders who are self-serving for their personal gain – that is clearly not the right attitude.

Leaders demonstrate Respect for themselves as they arrive to the understanding that they must nourish their capacity to lead by maintaining their health, establishing a life-long learning attitude, demonstrating self-management skills, and managing financial resources, to name a few. We discussed this earlier when we talked about inner-development. In other words, Respect for one's self is to understand the right way to treat one's self. In essence, effective leadership depends on your ability to first Honor & Respect yourself.

THE ELLISON MODEL TECHNIQUES

When teaching The Model, varied approaches referred to as techniques have been developed over the years to accommodate the learning process of particular fields and industries. These teaching techniques consistently use a three-part approach to communicate a beginning, middle, and end to each part of the process. The techniques include the teaching-learning process for interpersonal growth as well as leadership and character development within business, education, government, and faith-based organizations. The Ellison Model techniques are:

1. Diversity-Unity-Community
2. Content-Process-Product
3. Information-Knowledge-Wisdom
4. Ineffectual-Shallow-Effectual
5. Body-Soul-Spirit
6. Carnal-Emotional-Spiritual
7. Community Moment-Teachable Second-Sustainable Teachable Second
8. Reconciliation-Restoration-Sustainability
9. Buying-Selling-Distribution

For example, "in the education setting, the most commonly used techniques are content-process-product or diversity-unity-community. On the other hand, body-soul-spirit or carnal-emotional-spiritual might be best suited in faith-based settings" (Hunt, 2000). When we combine our inner-development, the intrinsic qualities bolstered by The Model, and the tangible results of engagement with self and others, we see the flow of the techniques play out in a continuous cycle. The *flow* articulates the constant transition and development of all organisms in the leadership development process. We are always moving from ineffectual, shallow, to effectual, and we are always moving from the stage of gaining information, to accessing knowledge, to utilizing it with wisdom. While this book is not considered a faith-based text, I still see the value in The Ellison Model technique of body-soul-spirit, particularly as we discuss external and internal values that serve as motivators in our human interaction for survival. On the other hand, when discussing conflict resolution, it is important to begin with reconciliation, move to restoration, and finalize the process with sustainable cornerstones to the once broken relationship. We *flow* in and out of these techniques everyday as we engage others and ourselves on social, political, economic, religious, and inter-personal levels. Along the way, many contributors, including both external and internal forces, mentor us.

Hunt and Ritchey (2000) described the following three levels of interaction as follows:

"At *Level One*, the individual is likely to have just come from the outer-circle of the Circular Diagram. In this case the individual must become acclimated with the inner-circle. The person may still be focused on their individual differences at this stage.

At *Level Two*, a mentor is a significant personality since they are recognized by the mentee as a guide who helps to facilitate the mentee's continual growth and development throughout the community building process. More importantly, the mentee comes to several realities: a) they recognize their own potential as a mentor, b) they begin to understand that everyone is a mentee and mentor, at once – concurrent learners and dispensers of knowledge, and c) the mentor is not always another person, it might be the conscience.

At *Level Three*, an enlarged body of mentors, who share the same goal, the same vision, and the same desire for mankind, experiences the outcome of an inclusive community. The inclusive community continues to grow as others, now as mature mentors, assume their responsibility to go to the outer-circle to bring others into the inner-circle."

KEYWORDS OF THE ELLISON MODEL

The Ellison Model maintains consistent language throughout all of its components. The following are a list of keywords used as building blocks and reinforced throughout the model:

- inclusive community building
- variety, oneness, shared vision
- honor, respect, and trust
- care, share, love
- character development
- GOMA
- ABCD
- goal, objective, method, attitude
- attitude, behavior, communication, discipline
- business, government, education, and religion
- solutions
- leadership
- bridge
- harmony
-

- foci
- inclusion
- mentorship
- relationship building
- conflict resolution
- multicultural appreciation
- economic development
- Hunt's Theorem
- solve problems/resolve conflicts
- vectors of conflict
- fear
- dishonesty
- disrespect
- disunity
- discommunity
- animosity

Reflective Journal Moment

6. Recall a moment when you have used any of the perspectives from the vector of conflict to create an adversarial relationship between yourself and another individual. Was the person aware of how you felt? Have you ever taken steps to resolve this conflict beginning with yourself and your perspective?

7. Recall a time when you have operated from the outer-circle and were able to move the situation into the inner-circle.

8. If diversity is only a starting point, what steps can you take to move from diversity to unity to community? Consider this question in either the sphere of your professional life or personal life. Would the steps of moving from diversity to unity to community look different in your personal than your professional life?

COLE'S LEADERSHIP -SOLUTION BRIDGE

Chapter 4

"The universe is so well balanced that the mere fact that you have a problem also serves as a sign that there is a solution." – Steve Maraboli, Life-changing Speaker, Bestselling Author, and Behavioral Scientist.

No truer words have been spoken for the leaders of our time than those by creator of The Ellison Model, Dr. Hunt, who on numerous occasions have said, "It's not the problem that counts, it's the solution." Problems surround us daily. The political, social, economic, religious, and personal experiences we each encounter continuously present its unique, yet, interrelated set of problems. If the world is constantly impacted by problems or conflict, then living a solution-oriented life is a daily process.

I define problems as a set of circumstances that create a temporary roadblock or challenge to achieving a **goal**. Problems, no matter the scope or breadth, also occur when the **objectives**, **methods**, or **attitudes** of individuals or groups **do not align** within the relationship they have with others or self. Some problems are more intricate than others and require several layers of solutions to arrive to alignment between parties. Note that problems do not necessarily indicate a conflict. I define conflict as use of the problem as a gateway to demonstrate disparaging or prejudice attitudes and behaviors toward others who share diverse perspectives. In using this definition, conflict occurs when individuals negatively use their vector of diversity as a basis for responding to a problem. While we may all encounter problems on a daily basis, the disposition of heart in approaching the solution to the problem determines whether or not it is a conflict.

Consider the following analogy: the radiator with the slow leak that caused the car to overheat was brought into the mechanic for repair. Within days of getting the car back the same problem resurfaced, causing the car to overheat at the most inconvenient time. Having a broken radiator is a problem that in most cases needs to be solved. If dissatisfaction with the mechanic now leads to a rant about the cultural background of the mechanic and how you dislike people from that particular nationality, then we can clearly see you have a conflict. Take note that the problem of the improperly fixed radiator is not the nucleus of the disparaging remarks; it simply became the justification to reveal your true disposition of heart regarding a particular group of people.

Let's look at another analogy. Departments are often asked to reasonably accomplish projects or programs with less than adequate budgets or staff. Being underfunded and understaffed is problematic. However, the *why* and *how* of the matter determines if it is a conflict. First, *why* are leaders choosing to underfund and understaff the department; and second, *how* are leaders responding to the issue of underfunding and understaffing? Underfunding and understaffing may exist because the company is not generating enough revenue to address those needs. Also, while revenue may grow, other needs may have been determined as more pertinent. That is understandable. However, if the powers that be see underfunding and understaffing as an opportunity for retaliation to individuals in the department, as a means to create a rational that leads to leadership changes, or based on personal feelings of animosity or friction amongst colleagues, then we clearly have a conflict at hand. We will always find conflict whenever the individual's disposition of heart is not aligned to inclusion, multicultural appreciation, mentorship, conflict resolution, and relationship building. According to the Circular Diagram on Community Building, the powers that be are operating in a counterclockwise position from the outer-circle, which is motivated by fear, distrust, and dishonor. According to the GOMABCD 7-Step Process, the powers that be need to make the right turn toward community building.

Conflict does not occur on its own; it has to be conflated by an individual or group on the basis of differences or distinctions created between themselves and others. In the above analogies, the improperly repaired car was used to make a distinction between the mechanic and themselves based on nationality. Regarding the matter of funding and staffing, the powers that be could have made a distinction based on any number of factors, such as feeling that an individual is rude because they do no say "good morning" to having a personal dislike for seeing certain genders or ethnicities in leadership positions.

COLE'S LEADERSHIP-SOLUTION BRIDGE CONCEPT

Leadership

Problem

Solution

Fig. 8

As an emerging leader during my undergraduate collegiate years, David Cole, my mentor and advisor, advised me daily on how to be a solution-oriented leader. The insight gained from our many reflective conversations at the FIU Biscayne Bay Campus left a lasting impression on me. David emphasized that in the role as a leader, one must have must focus on addressing the issues of social justice, human rights, and understanding the social construct of the world around us. Coupled with the on-going trainings of The Ellison Model from Dr. Hunt through conferences, workshops, and seminars, my interactions with David allowed me to see many aspects of the leadership development process. Specifically, I observed the importance of the leader serving as the middle man or go between of problems and solutions or conflicts and resolutions. Leaders are the bridge. When facing a problem, the best-case scenario is that leaders bridge their followers toward a solution. While the outward behavior of conflict may be seen between two individuals or groups, the greater problem is the (personal or inner-) conflict of the involved parties. The internal conflict of the involved leaders must first be resolved before they can bridge the problem to a solution. In other words, leaders must first bridge their personal or inner-conflict to a solution before they can effectively do so for others. However, the leader's responsibility is to always serve as a bridge for their sphere of influence beginning with their inner conflict and then moving externally to group and community conflict.

By holding out your left and right hands, palms facing up, you can see a visual representation of the Leadership-Solution Bridge. What is on the left hand? The problem/conflict. What is on the right hand? The solution. What do you notice occupying the space between your left and right hands? The answer is *you*. Individuals, whether personal or within corporations or organizations, are the leaders who bridge themselves and their sphere of influence from the problem to a solution. Whether the Bering Strait, a telephone, Skype, or lunch meeting, it has always taken a bridge to make connections. A bridge is a connecting device that facilitates progress, and leadership is the act of bridging a problem to a solution or a conflict to a resolution. Leaders make these daily connections by moving people and organizations across their leadership bridge.

The accountability measures inherent to The Ellison Model forces leaders to introspectively critique their motivation, attitude, and behaviors according to The Ellison Model's "Way of Life." This is critical because leaders must resolve their inner-conflict, such as biases, stereotypes, fears, and traditional perspectives, if flawed, in order to effectively lead. In each step of the process, as a bridge is often centered over water, leaders have the opportunity to reflect, learn, and adjust the manner in which they are building inclusive community. And where practices that counter The Ellison Model are found, they have the opportunity to toss those motivations, attitudes, and behaviors overboard. Under your leadership bridge is an ever-expanding universe of hope, support, and development that allows past shortcomings to be "water under the bridge" as leaders are willing to embrace the model.

The Cole's Leadership-Solution Bridge is a simple concept to remind emerging leaders of who they are in the leadership process. The bridge's design and construction will vary in presentation based on an individual's personality and perception of the problem, but not in principle. The Ellison Model approach deploys several components, as previously described, to help leaders build and reinforce their leadership bridge free of conflict and bias attitudes that would otherwise earmark roadblocks or stagnation in the process.

Types of Leaders

As previously stated, individuals enact leadership on a daily basis. However, I personally sum the quality of leadership into two categories irrespective of style or skills: basic leadership and inclusive leadership.

"Basic leaders" pursue happiness. Basic leaders are self-motivated for personal gain, compromise the process, and lack ethics – they are what Hunt refers to as dis-community builders. When "basic leadership" is deployed, individuals' exclusive behaviors reflect their attitude. At that moment, their vertical relationship rotates the relationship building process backwards toward dis-community. Meaning, the leader is more concerned about "appearing" as Caring, Sharing, and Loving than they are about truly developing a sense of self that reflects Trust, Honor, and Respect for self and others. An individual may take all the necessary steps to acquire a desired leadership position including shaking hands, kissing babies, meeting quotas, earning high evaluation markings, networking with management, or dressing extremely appropriate for the work environment. These behaviorally driven demonstrations are a pretense of a caring, sharing, and loving attitude.

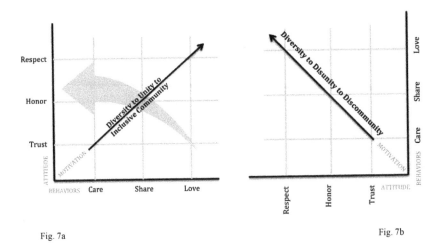

Fig. 7a

Fig. 7b

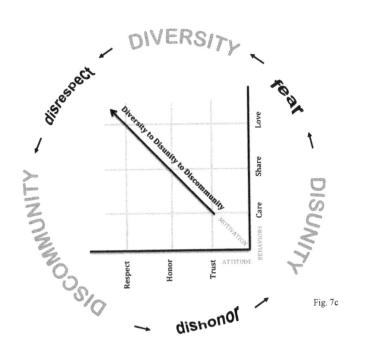

Fig. 7c

However, upon acquisition of the position, the qualities of a basic leader kick in to reveal the individual's motivation was always self-centered. Inclusive leaders do not pursue happiness – they pursue solutions. Arrival to the right solution invariably makes leaders happy with the outcome, but the guiding motivation should always be to solve the problem or resolve the conflict in an inclusive community-building attitude that reflects principles such as those found within The Ellison Model. In pursuit of any goal, inclusive leaders transform their sphere of influence by demonstrating and promoting inclusive community building characteristics. Leaders throughout history have pursued solutions to problems and conflicts (i.e. prejudice, social injustice, racism, infringement on human rights, and the status quo, to name a few). Many of these leaders felt a deep calling, a hunger and thirst for the fair treatment of the collective community, which led to the pursuit of solutions to overcome oppressive systems.

Inclusive leaders seize opportunities to solve problems. They pursue a role (not a position or title) to effectively find solutions. Inclusive leadership deploys solution-oriented practices that utilize various leadership styles and skills with an inclusive community building attitude; caring, sharing, and loving behaviors; affirming communication; and a disciplined demeanor to arrive at favorable solutions for the purpose of the collective. Inclusive leaders move their sphere of influence from diversity, to unity, to an inclusive community.

Followship versus Leadership

The first responsibility of a leader is to follow. I have often heard people instruct others to not be a follower. Being a follower usually carries a negative connotation, implying that others think for you or easily influences your actions. It is also common thinking that being a follower makes you subordinate to another person. After all, if you are in charge, as the final decision maker and person being held most accountable, why then should you allow yourself to "follow" another person? But in one form or another, everyone is a follower. Everyone is influenced by an internal or external host that helps to develop or diminish who they are. The question is: who or what are you following?

Inclusive leaders understand the necessity and complimentary nature of following and leading. Following and leading is a symbiotic relationship. Inclusive leaders model proper followship by following a set of guiding principles that supports the way they lead; leaders follow the rules, the same rules that is expected of those they lead; and leaders also follow the assessment and expertise of their counterparts and colleagues. Leadership and followship are no different from the mentor-mentee exchange wherein the mentor and mentee often exchange roles in the learning-teaching process. While we acknowledge that one may have legitimate power through their stated position, the relationship can only be successful if all parties allow space for leading and following as deemed appropriate. We can therefore acknowledge a leader-follower exchange amongst all stakeholders in a group setting.

Followers also lead other followers in the leader-follower exchange. For example, if Subordinate X decides they disagree with Leader W, Subordinate X may sway others into further disagreement against Leader W. Albeit Leader W may hold the ranking position of authority, Subordinate X has a level of influence over her counterparts, which, in effect means she has a certain level of referent power. That power makes her a leader amongst her peers. Following is not a bad thing, in spite of the stigma it may receive. Following is a necessary part of the leadership process as we follow guiding principles and exchange our roles for the growth and development of the community at-large or the communities we serve.

It's Not the Problem That Counts (Poem)

In addition to my role as a leadership development trainer and conflict resolution practitioner, I am also a poet and spoken word artist. Most of my poetry is a critique on our social world highlighting problems and conflicts I've observed in gender roles, the male identity, sexuality, and religion. To date I have published three books of poetry. My poetry also speaks to personal development through which I seek to empower listeners and readers toward overcoming obstacles. I dub my poems as "powertry." One such piece is the poem "It's Not the Problem That Counts" (Carter, 2014), adapted from

Hunt's creative works as a playwright and songwriter. The poem takes a mathematical approach to reinforce the maxim, "It's not the problem that counts, it's the solution."

Problems don't count
They're not mathematically inclined
Problems can't composite
They're too busy being prime
-marily the focus
Hoping you'll cosine
Going off on tangents
Through vectors of conflict lines

Problems have a standard deviation
From resolving situations
Problems carry combinations
With inaccurate approximations
Like misery loves company
Tries to form triangulations
Problems don't count
They're trapezoids of dilation

Problems don't see how I've grown
It thinks I'm weak but I am strong
I know where Problems went wrong
For even shorthand division is long

Standing firm in your perfection
How you hate rejection
Not seeing your regression
Where problems rule, I'm the exception.

Solution is a numberer
It calculates concise
Solution understands the commutative property
Of multiplication in human life
Knowing there's a plane

To sum the difference of contention
Methods to alleviate poverty
Is its exponential function.

Solution has the transitive property
Of building inclusion properly
Solution negates the animosity
And compounds the possibility
To rightfully divide
And increase the probability
Solution loves to count
You into every opportunity

We have come to this conclusion
The answer is not exclusion
The solution is inclusion
Not evolution; it's revolution.

Reflective Journal Moment

9. Recall a moment when you used a problem to create conflict between yourself and others. What did you do and what would you do differently?

10. Recall a moment when you bridged a problem to a solution or a conflict to resolution. What was the problem/conflict and what steps did you take to be the bridge?

EMERGING

AS THE RIGHT PERSON IN THE RIGHT PLACE AT THE RIGHT TIME

Chapter 5

"And those who were seen dancing were thought to be insane by those who could not hear the music." – Friedrich Nietzsche, 19th century German philosopher

Your journey toward understanding who you are and embracing your purpose may sometimes look strange to others. Often, it is a vision that only you can see; a drum beat to which you are dancing that no one else seems to hear. Still I encourage you to keep dancing. Keep evolving. Keep emerging. According to the Merriam-Webster dictionary, to emerge means "to become manifest, to come out into, to rise from an obscure or inferior position or condition, or to come into being through evolution." These are beautiful definitions that acknowledge the undertaking of a process that produces an outcome. The application of inclusion, multicultural appreciation, conflict resolution, mentorship, and relationship building is a revolutionary process with promise of sustainable outcomes. The process brings the individual to a space of leadership, where trust, honor, respect, caring, sharing, and loving behaviors are demonstrated for the purpose of building an inclusive community. The enactment of leadership in positive character and in manifest behaviors is what can be expected.

Dreams are often associated with lofty goals or maybe aspirations of a financially abundant life. Sometimes we dream of going to exotic places or having certain euphoric or adventuresome experiences. There's nothing wrong with having dreams. Embrace them. However, we should allow purpose to drive our dreams, not the other way around. Purpose is the culmination of your best self curated with certain abilities unique to you for a particular space and time. You can be purposed for multiple things, but most importantly, your purpose speaks to your truest self and the value you bring to your sphere of influence. Psychiatrist Melvin Rubenstein (1961) wrote the following about purpose:

> A patient who speaks of having no purpose in life is usually referring to the fact that his behavior is not consciously, intensely motivated, so that he is constantly faced with the bleak prospect of nongratification. Real gratification can occur only from the heightened feeling that comes with carrying out purpose. Without purpose there is no heightened feeling thus no chance of gratification.

What Rubenstein describes as gratification, I refer to as a sense of accomplishment in this text. Discovering your purpose is its own process, which sometimes may include rediscovery or discovering a new purpose appropriate to a new space and time in your life. You may sometimes have a specific purpose for a moment in time for a specific situation. However, your life purpose or one's overall (meta) purpose on planet earth will be a constant, unchanging beacon that guides you with synergy and alignment. Your purpose may not garner you monetary wealth, but there is bountiful wealth in other areas of life. Being in good health, having reliable friends and family, access to people of influence, and having great critical thinking skills, a solution-oriented mindset, a growth mindset, and great writing and publicly speaking skills are all forms of wealth. Adopting models, theories, and practices that develop your character development, promotes inclusion, and helps to shape your attitude and perspective are also forms of wealth.

Without oversimplifying purpose, you will notice that there are skillsets that you seem to naturally have. Your purpose is often found in these skillsets. You might be passionate about a certain cause. The passion may have been developed through your personal experience or the experience of someone close to you, but your purpose is often found in your passion. Your purpose may be recognized after years of training and learning a particular craft or industry. Suddenly, planned or unplanned, you have become an authority or influencer in a particular area. Your input and contribution to the industry grows indispensable, finding purpose in the seniority and reputation you have acquired in that specific industry. As an artist, educator, engineer, athletic coach, activist, parent, or any other role you may play, it might not garner you monetary wealth. Nonetheless, leading a purpose-driven life provides a sense of peace and satisfaction. It also best positions you to emerge as the right person, in the right place, at the right time.

Right Person. Right Place. Right Time.

I admit, it sounds like a tall order. It almost sounds too perfect; too good to be true. It seems to remove room for human error when we know human beings make mistakes. How then is it possible to be the right person, in the right place, at the right time – and dare I say, all the time. The answer is not a complicated one, but it is also not to be oversimplified. Emerging as the right person, in the right place, at the right time is a life-long learning process that requires continuous work, introspection, and evolution. This rightness of person includes "mistakes" in the life-long curriculum for learning and growing in order to learn from them, minimize them, and teach others from them.

The Ellison Model and the available body of leadership development resources provide you the opportunity to emerge as the right person in the right place at the right time – every time – when you have the *right* **attitude**. Sociologist Read Bain (1928) reviewed the definitions of attitude offered by other researchers in his article *An Attitude on Attitude Research*. Bain summarizes Thomas & Znaniecki (1918) definition of attitude to be "the subjective reaction to a value." P. M. Symonds (1925) identified seven uses of the term attitude: 1) great organic drives (motives), 2) muscular set, 3) generalized conduct, 4) neural set or readiness to adjust, 5) emotional concomitant of action, 6) feeling concomitant of action, and 7) accepting or rejecting verbal responses. Bain concludes, "Perhaps the most common, and, to the writer, the most indefensible, use of the term [attitude] identifies it with opinion as revealed by verbal responses" (p. 944). As such, an individual's verbal response is often viewed as an indication of their perspective. This is not always accurate, nonetheless, attitude consists of multiple meanings that all culminate into a certain energy given to the problem or conflict, often times unstated. The energy derived from an individual's attitude either helps to resolve or exacerbate the issue. Energy provides the necessary power to create motion, also referred to as motivation. Put otherwise, what is motivating the person's response to a situation? Attitudes can be motivated by a handful of factors from the Vectors of Conflict table, a general lack of honor, trust, and respect for others, or a competitive nature fueled by discommunity building factors. Additionally, while an individual's attitude may be a subjective response (Thomas, 1918), it's not an arbitrary response. Attitude is impacted by the quality of the relationship we have with others derived from the stated or unstated purpose of the relationship.

By having the *right* attitude, I am not speaking specifically of having a pleasant demeanor that appears to not be combative. Neither am I speaking of *'being nice'* to others. While being nice certainly goes a long way, I do not wish to confuse attitude with the outward display of an individual's behavior toward others. Hunt (2006) defines attitude as first and foremost a disposition of the individual's heart. Attitude relates more with the individual's intrinsic value system that guides their behavior, communication, and discipline than with their demonstrative behavior.

As seen in the GOMABCD 7-Step Process, the *right* attitude makes the right turn toward an inclusive community building solution when placed into any given situation. The *right* attitude is also agreement with the appropriateness of response to a situation, which ought to commensurate with the level of importance or urgency of the situation. Responses to most situations involve knowing the important difference between when to speak and when to actively listen. Despite the response to the circumstance, whether delayed or immediate, the disposition of heart should always be centered on a community building solution that demonstrates the principles of The Ellison Model, whether in the boardroom or the classroom, on the field or in the home. While the tone and word choice of our communication are vital in shaping relationships, we must also understand that the synergy of tone of voice, word choice, understanding your audience, and understanding the dynamics of the situation is a learning process, which over time, develops an exemplary leader with increasingly more tactfulness.

The greater challenge may appear when individuals fail to properly understand and decipher between personality types versus disposition of heart; in which case, individuals may sometimes prefer to work with personality types they find more complimentary to their own. As a consequence, the input of those who do not have a personality match might be overlooked—a form of exclusion, whether purposely or incidentally. From such miscalculation, problems can emerge. Note, however, understanding the personality type of your stakeholders, audience, or those you are accountable for will go a tremendously long way in building relationships and maximizing their contribution. Personality type tests are often conducted in human resource/staff development training, leadership development workshops, or retreats for executive boards members, managers, and student leaders. Popular personality type tests include the Myers-Briggs Type Indicator, created in 1943, and the Carl Jung Typology test first published in 1921. Unfortunately, personality types do not reflect disposition of heart. The *right* disposition of heart is available to any personality type; whoever decides to embrace it. In fact, I am of the school of thought that varied personality types in a group setting helps to vary the lenses through which we interact and make binding decisions.

The **Right** Person is the individual with the *right* attitude. The *right* attitude means the leader is willing to uphold the inclusive community building process by sharing resources. Resources may include financial capital, time, personnel, knowledge and information, or equipment. These and other resources are available to assist in reaching the goal. The goal may involve resolving an internal department conflict or enhancing a program-coordinated effort. The owner or manager of these resources can be seen as the mentor. In the situation where an individual imparts to others, they become the mentor, and the recipients are the mentee. As the *right* attitude results in a willingness to share, the steward of the resources becomes a part of the mentor-mentee exchange.

The **Right** Place is not a physical location. Place speaks to the level of maturity to which the leader has arrived, wherein they are willing to share their resources. In the place of maturity, people are more interested in giving than harboring resources for themselves. In an extreme situation of conflict, the mature leader has arrived to a place in which they do not compromise their inclusive community building ethics for personal gain nor are they seduced by discommunity building agents.

The **Right** Time includes the daily opportunities presented to the leader to demonstrate his or her maturity and leadership ability in a manner that cares, shares, loves, trusts, honors, and respects the stakeholders in their sphere of influence. In the leadership hemisphere, you can make any time the *right* time to do the *right* thing. You always have a right to question the ethics, purpose, or means of practice—ensure the *right* attitude—in an effort to ensure community building compliance. When then is the *right* time to emerge? The *right* time is always **now**.

To recap, 1) the *right* attitude steers the problem or conflict toward an inclusive community building solution and 2) maintains the appropriate response to said problem or conflict. If attitude is the cornerstone for both intrinsic and extrinsic behaviors, from whence does attitude generate? As mentioned before, according to The Ellison Model, attitude is reflected in the disposition of the heart. Hunt (2006) wrote the following about attitude in his Government of the Bahamas Urban Renewal training manual:

> The right Attitude is the starting point in any successful urban renewal training because attitude reflects how people feel or think about what is presented to them. A person's attitude is influenced by a number of factors among which are their perceptions of whether those seeking to renew them believe in their renewal. It is therefore critical that the mentor leaves no doubt in the minds of the people that he/she fully endorses their renewal. This is not done only by words alone because people say one thing but do another; renewal must be demonstrated in the personal character of the mentors. (The ABCD's of Character Development and Urban Renewal Proposal, International Library)

As described by Hunt, the attitude of the stakeholders is impacted by the attitude of the leadership. With a history of corruption, self-interest, and a growing gap between the haves and the have-nots, trust between the people we serve and the leaders who (do no) serve them has eroded over the years, decades, and centuries. This has made the communities skeptical of those with good intentions and heart-felt service. It can sometimes be an uphill battle when attempting to restore trust with and within the community because people understand that the world systems of government, business, religion, and education have not always been impartial. As you see, there has always been an urgent need for the emergence of leaders with the *right* attitude, behavior, communication and discipline to reestablish the care, share, love, trust, honor, and respect between leaders and stakeholders. Emerging as the rightness of person, place, and time does not solve all problems at once, but it establishes the pathway of your reputation within the community. While community stakeholders may feel failed by the perception of "the system," they can get to know you as a reliable, trustworthy resource in the interim. All sectors of life is in need of renewal, whether social, political, religious, psychological, or economical. Like revolution, which means to make a full rotation back to its original starting point, renewal means to re-new or return back to the condition of being operable in its originally intended state. When you consider the rise of problems or conflicts, it means that some element in the environment has moved out of place, and needs to be readjusted into alignment. Your emergence in this space can and is the difference needed for renewal, or put another way, needed for survival.

In the words of Dawn Burgher: A Story on Using The Ellison Model

Dawn Burgher, administrative manager in the financial services industry, was faced with interpersonal and cultural conflicts in her department. Being trained on The Ellison Model for years, she relied on her community building paradigm shift to find and implement strategic solutions. While she emerged as the right person in the right place at the right time for herself and her staff, it took time and consistency over a period of years to cement its effectiveness.

"When I joined the organization in April 2007, I was one of two African-American managers who were responsible for driving revenue growth and ensuring compliance with policies and processes that impact audit results. The folks I was called to lead were predominately Caucasian. I was accused of having racial biases and being exclusive in my outlook.

Understanding The Ellison Model and that it was not just a philosophical or academic framework, I implemented a Diversity and Inclusion Luncheon that occurred just around the Thanksgiving Holiday. This was a welcomed idea as the firm at the time mandated that each employee complete at least two diversity activities annually. The luncheon was the perfect solution for each employee to achieve one of those requirements with minimal effort.

For the luncheon, each employee was asked to contribute a dish that represented their culture or a culture with which they identified. The dish was displayed with the flag of the country and the name of the dish. The room was decorated with a diversity theme with colors and flags from different countries. The employees gathered in the conference room for the luncheon – one of the very few occasions all employees voluntarily ate lunch together. On the program, I made a very short cultural presentation, which included participation from others to also share things from their culture. Also on the program was a short speech on diversity. During that speech I shared that when diversity is seen as different we are already beginning at a place of conflict; however, when diversity is viewed as variety it prepares each person's heart to be more welcoming of the others and thus we are able to begin from a place of togetherness. This seemingly simple statement was so impactful to my manager that he took the concept "diversity should not be seen as different but as variety" to the CEO of the organization and to the Human Resources Department.

The luncheon has been occurring since 2007 and the community of my staff and colleagues has transformed in a very positive way. I'm happy I did not focus on the statement of others that I was racially bias (the problem), but on the principles of The Ellison Model and its guidance on inclusion and multicultural appreciation (the solution)."

Dawn's ending remark that she did not focus on the statement of others that accused her of being racially bias made a tremendous difference because it revealed her disposition of heart. She was not focused on the problem more heavily than the solution. Equally important was that Dawn saw herself as a mentor responsible for teaching others how to move from diversity, to unity, to community. Dawn demonstrated her rightness of person, place, and time through her awareness of self as a mentor, maturity to remain focused on a solution, and program implementation for compliance with the company's diversity activity requirements that also helped to build an inclusive community in her work environment. Her inclusive community building efforts paid further dividends, as her manager was able to share her remarks up the corporate hierarchy.

Social Homeostasis

In 2010, U.S. swimmer Fran Crippen died during a 10-kilometer marathon in the United Arab Emirates (CNN, 2010). His cause of death was cited as muscle fatigue and a heart attack. Doctors said the fatigue was caused by the warmness of the water. The water temperature was estimated to be about 87 degrees. According to the CNN article, Ken Kamler, a doctor and author who explores survival in extreme circumstances said the body dissipates heat through the skin during swims, and when that water is warm, "it's hard for your body to get rid of the heat." In another story, NBC News (2016) reported Fourteen-year-old Cameron Gosling died from cold-water shock after jumping into the River Wear, just outside of Durham, England, back in July 2015.

The human body's core temperature of 98.6 degrees F/37 degrees C can neither drop too fast, resulting in hypothermia, or on the other hand, the human body's temperature cannot raise too quickly, which may result in overheating. The body's inability to regulate its temperature in the proper amount of time can result in fatigue, fainting, sleepiness, clumsiness, confusion, slurred speech, shaking, and sometimes death. The change in temperature can shock the body and send it into a state of temporary paralysis. To avoid these effects, the body goes through different ranges in an effort to get back to its normative state—the body is seeking to establish homeostasis. The term homeostasis, coined by physician Walter Cannon in 1930, is defined as a stabilizing function that the body takes on in order to survive. The term has since been used to also represent social, cultural, economic, and political systems as well.

I believe the systems of our social world have experienced shock after shock and have ping-ponged in and out of paralysis for centuries through sweeping devastations such as wars, slavery, genocide, gentrification, natural disasters, caste systems, capitalism, colonialism, and terrorism amongst other things. While these devastations reflect our world at-large, they first stem from our local interactions with individuals and our internalized conflict with self. It has been historically evidenced that individuals have first imposed a microcosm of enslavement, caste systems, colonialism, and gentrification of other individual's physical, emotional, financial, and psychological well-being through their interpersonal interactions long before it ballooned into our larger society. The current state of systems created by human beings demand a renewal in order to reestablish (what I dub as) social homeostasis. Social homeostasis speaks to the equilibrium (community building) of human interaction in all sectors of our world system, including education, government, business, faith-based, and inter-personal. The same manner in which homeostasis defines the human body's need to maintain balance, our social interaction, as human beings, also demands the same. As the human body, on its own, instinctively fights to establish balance for the sake of survival, the human being in our social world has always instinctively taken leadership to combat injustice through its fight for human and civil rights.

Problems and conflicts, which lead to both minor and major injustices (discommunity building), mean that the interaction between human beings are no longer in alignment with the same goals, objectives, methods, and attitude. At this juncture, renewal, or revolution, or movement back to a regulated balance or equilibrium of peace, understanding, and inclusion needs to reoccur. This is why emergence of the rightness of person, place, and time is so critical in the 21st century. Having an inclusive community building attitude is the difference maker. Your emergence happens over time, circumstance by circumstance. Yet, in each situation there is an opportunity to emerge as an Ellison Model agent with the *right* attitude. You may not physically see immediate results in your sphere of influence. However, maintaining the *right* attitude over time will ensure your manifestation into The Ellison Model change agent that you already are, just waiting to emerge.

Tips for Leaders in the 21st Century

I was afforded the opportunity to supervise departments, manage and allocate multi-million dollar budgets, serve on multiple internal and community committees, and implement new processes amongst many more experiences as a student leader and young professional. In the midst of it all, I have made numerous mistakes and missed opportunities to propel my personal development and career. This should come as no surprise, seeing how leadership development comes with challenges. Leadership is a learning process by design and learning from your mistakes is one of the greatest gifts in the process. The following are some personal tips on leadership for emerging leaders in our 21st century and beyond:

Entrepreneurship: Embrace the entrepreneur in you, even on your 9-5 job. The fast pace of information and global integration through the Internet and social media present several opportunities for innovation and economic growth. It requires an active search, but opportunities are there.

Passion: Discovering your passion may take time, and that is okay. As you progress in your career, you will be afforded opportunities to serve in various roles that allow you to simultaneously learn new things about yourself and develop/improve your skills. Discover your passion and then wisely pursue it.

The Ellison Model: Adopt The Ellison Model as a way of life. Allow these community building principles to guide your motivations, attitude, and behavior. The principles of The Ellison Model do a great job of holding you accountable while empowering you to create the win-win-win--a personal win, professional win, and community win.

Life-long Learning: It is important to adopt a lifestyle of life-long learning across multiple topics and platforms. Learning may occur through mentorship, formal and informal education, certifications, books, conferences, and local, national, and international news to name a few. You will discover the interconnectedness of our world as you learn about various people, places, and things. Study to show yourself approved.

Mentorship: Surround yourself with like-minded community building individuals, who support your personal, emotional, and social well-being and overall development. This includes who you select as a mentor, friend, and even as a life partner. These close contacts will help to focus you and collectively build an inclusive community. On the other hand, if you are not watchful, those same individuals might distract you from your purpose.

Reflective Journal Moment

11. In what scenarios have you seen yourself emerge as the right person, in the right place, at the right time? In what area (person, place, or time) were you the strongest? In what area do observe a need for growth?

12. If money were not an obstacle, how would you contribute to improving society?

Part II

for the emerging mentor, advisor, and supervising manager

HUNT'S EXPERIENTIAL LEADERSHIP PROCESS

Chapter 6

"Tell me and I forget, teach me and I may remember, involve me and I learn." – *Benjamin Franklin*

Leadership development for emerging leaders occurs in the learning and working environment through meaningful and intentional experiences. Such experiences cultivate leadership similar to how constant engagement or stimulation develops the muscles in our bodies, where failure to stimulate or exercise the muscle may result in atrophy. In the leadership development process, atrophy presents itself as apathy or stagnation. Where leadership is concerned, effective mentorship is a meaningful guard against the potential for underdeveloped muscles. Mentors may appear through a supervising manager, academic advisor, or someone identified specifically as a mentor. People are also mentored through indirect mediums such as radio, television, and social media outlets. Mentors help to guide and shape the mentees' thinking and problem solving abilities. Everyone has a mentor or a collection of mentors in one form or the other. Whether or not someone has agreed to formally serve as a mentor does not dilute the impact we may have on others. Subsequently, the disposition of heart of mentors must also be inclusive-minded and community oriented. Emerging as the mentor, in a direct or indirect role, also constitutes the rightness of person, place, and time.

Mentorship

Mentorship consists of formal relationships between entities that have an official capacity over people who serve under their administration, such as a teacher and students, clergy person and followers, or supervisor and subordinates. Mentorship also consists of informal relationships that engage individuals in a less direct, but not necessarily unobvious way, such as relationships amongst friends, siblings, and counterparts in the workplace. One thing that is for sure is mentorship cuts across every sector and level of interaction throughout life. The passing on of ways and customs in our environment, broad or narrow, whether through organizational culture, home life, or religious persuasion, is rooted in the exchange of information reflected through the attitude, behavior, and types of communications we incur. The exchange is a type of mentorship. In effect, our human race is set in a cycle of mentoring in which we all simultaneously teach and learn, resulting in an inflection and reflection of the world around us. The results are very simple: we live in the world we create and continue to recreate. What we are therefore hoping for are mentors who demonstrate the care, share, love, trust, respect, and honor needed to positively impact the lives of emerging leaders.

When looking at school age children and college students, for example, the impact of mentorship from positive role models results in ways that help reduce school dropout rates, increase academic achievement, promote self-identity and positive self-image, reduce risky behaviors, and facilitate career development (DuBois, Holloway, Valentine, & Cooper, 2002; Jacobi, 1991; Kram, 1985; Levinson et al., 1978). The same positives can be seen in the workplace with staff moral, longevity, and the promotion of self-identity and positive self-image amongst colleagues.

Within The Ellison Model framework, the mentor (advisor, managing supervisor, or coach) "promotes teaching and learning and reinforces to the mentee that they are just as valuable as the mentor" (Hoyt, 2013). The mentor dissolves the hierarchy of separation in an effort to be and demonstrate inclusivity. The mentor's role is to coordinate and direct experiences that foster the development of their mentee into exemplary leaders who emerge as the right person in the right place at the right time as the mentor simultaneously emerges. Note that being an emerging leader can happen at every level as the purview of leadership expands with broader and deeper responsibilities. Also, considering shifts that occur in systems or markets, the leadership style necessary at one point in time may become antiquated, positioning the leader into a new space of evolution. At this point, the updated leader needs to emerge as a renewed leader to qualitatively be the right person in the right place at the right time. With this understanding, years of experience, age, socio-economic status, and other vectors of perspective may play less of a role in the process of emergence. Being a billionaire, for instance, does not limit your capacity to learn and grow. In any case, the leader may need a guide to further enhance their leadership development.

While mentorship shows up in many ways, the je ne sais quoi of mentorship in the higher education student affairs sphere and the business/corporate setting, is the ability of mentors to assign or mentees to seek out tasks, roles, and responsibilities that specifically work to build the conglomerate of skills needed to lead in a group setting while promoting self-actualization. Similarly, the life coach practitioner is able to assist their clients identify the type of tasks, roles, and responsibilities needed to achieve their professional or entrepreneurial goals. These settings allow for the tangible, measurable, and intrinsic values to interplay at once. The Hunt Experiential Leadership Concept works to bolster and enhance the mentoring opportunities that exist in these settings.

HUNT'S EXPERIENTIAL LEADERSHIP PROCESS
A MENTOR'S GUIDE TO DEVELOPING LEADERS USING THE ELLISON MODEL

The Hunt Experiential Leadership Process (The HELP) was brainstormed from my personal experience as an undergraduate student in multiple leadership roles. The concept is written in honor of sociologist Deryl G. Hunt, Ph.D., who maintained and supported the point of view that individuals maximized their leadership potential when the environment engages them with meaningful responsibilities, real challenges, and real impact for a sustainable outcome. I was immersed with projects and roles that actualized the essence of this concept under Hunt's mentorship during my undergraduate collegiate years. Hunt has also demonstrated great humility in the development of his works. Specifically, he named The Ellison Model after a colleague instead of naming it after himself. In the same vein of humility, I honor the honorable by naming this concept after him—it is also fitting as the concept is adopted from The Ellison Model.

The Hunt Experiential Leadership Process (The HELP) can be tied to the Person-Environment Theory (Astin, 1984), which focuses on the depth, breadth and type of engagement with the environment. As research on student development continue to support that involvement in campus activities has a positive correlation with retention and academics (Kuh and Pike, 2005), how emerging leaders are mentored makes their engagement that much more meaningful. A study by Helen Ellison (2002) further evidenced The Ellison Model as a collegiate retention tool. The HELP assumes that all students have the potential to lead, and considers leadership as a muscle that develops through exercise. Exercise takes place with weights, resistance, impact, and repetition as illustrated in the graphic:

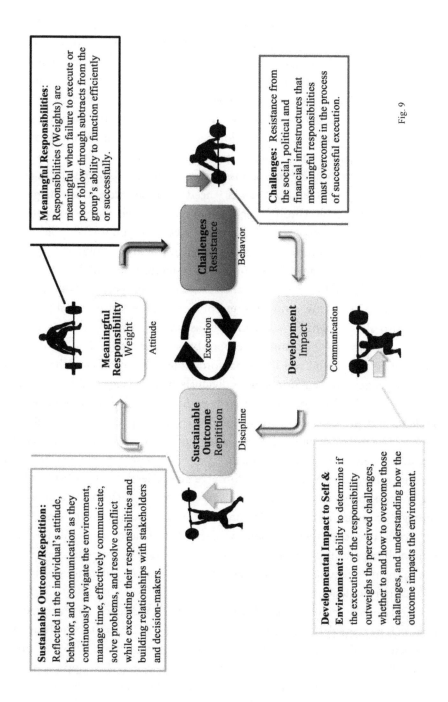

Meaningful Responsibilities: Responsibilities (Weights) are meaningful when failure to execute or poor follow through subtracts from the group's ability to function efficiently or successfully.

Challenges: Resistance from the social, political and financial infrastructures that meaningful responsibilities must overcome in the process of successful execution.

Sustainable Outcome/Repetition: Reflected in the individual's attitude, behavior, and communication as they continuously navigate the environment, manage time, effectively communicate, solve problems, and resolve conflict while executing their responsibilities and building relationships with stakeholders and decision-makers.

Developmental Impact to Self & Environment: ability to determine if the execution of the responsibility outweighs the perceived challenges, whether to and how to overcome those challenges, and understanding how the outcome impacts the environment.

Fig. 9

for the emerging mentor, advisor, and supervising manager

Development of the leadership muscle occurs through weight lifting. Results are met with weights intense enough to stimulate the muscles, making them fit enough to compete in leadership roles. Next, muscle memory is sustained through repetition. Nevitt Sanford (1969) defined development as "the organization of increasing complexity." Accordingly, once the muscle memory is sustained or becomes familiar with one level of intensity, more weight can be added for further development. Lastly, resistance occurs in both directions simultaneously from the push/pull (day-to-day inter-) action of weight training or meaningful responsibilities, which also develops the muscle.

In summary, emerging leaders need intense weight training for development to occur. Through such training with meaningful responsibilities, the environment is positively impacted resulting in improved policy and practices, organizational structure, organizational culture, specific departments, or programs. Furthermore, meaningful responsibilities supports the individual's need for validation and mattering (Schlossberg, 1989; Rendon, 1994), and in effect, gives students and professionals a sense of real purpose, which also allows them to see themselves as sincere members of the process. In the absence of meaningful responsibilities, emerging leaders do not encounter challenges or resistance. Sanford (1966) indicates that if there is too little challenge in the environment, individuals may feel safe and satisfied, but they do not develop (pp. 44-46); also, without meaningful responsibilities, students and professionals subsequently lack real purpose and are unable to equate their responsibilities to having real impact (a consequence or reward to the individuals and the environment). They also associate real impact with meaningful responsibilities as they "observe and reflect" (Kolb, 1984) on how the process personally impacts them as a result of their successful follow through or failure to execute. The impact on the emerging leader unveils: 1) the consequences they personally face for failure to execute their responsibilities, 2) the reward for successful execution of their responsibilities, and 3) the measureable effect of which their successes or failure to execute has on the environment.

Additionally, emerging leaders process their experience as described by Kolb's Experiential Learning Cycle, wherein they reflect and learn from the experience, and tryout what they have learned (Kolb, 1981, 1985). In other words, the mentees are afforded opportunities to refine their approach over time as they learn how to overcome resistance and resolve their inner-conflict. This is an ongoing process of continuous engagement, repetition, with meaningful responsibilities that establishes sustainable outcomes of an inclusive community building attitude, behavior, communication, and discipline within the mentees. The sustainable outcomes are the lessons learned in the process as emerging leaders are held accountable and given space to refine their approach to executing their responsibility.

The responsibility of the mentor (managers, advisors, supervisors, and coaches) is to help emerging leaders design and construct their leadership bridge through an experiential learning process that fosters the tenets of The Ellison Model.

Meaningful Responsibilities/Weights

Responsibilities are meaningful when failure to execute or poor follow through subtracts from the group's ability to function efficiently or successfully. Note that meaningful responsibilities will vary across institution and organization types. The following are some examples of responsibilities that are likely to have meaning:

- Assigned committee chair or project lead
- Assigned to create the meeting agenda
- Assigned to complete the project report
- Assigned as the fiscal manager for a project
- Assigned to design promotional material
- Assigned as staff developer to conduct training of new members or staff

Challenges/Resistance

Challenges are resistance from social, political and financial infrastructures that meaningful responsibilities must overcome in the process of successful execution of those responsibilities. The right amount of resistance is a necessary part of the development process as it forces emerging leaders to develop by finding creative (ethical) alternatives, persevering through the political climate, or fine tuning their overall approach. The following are types of challenges or resistance individuals may experience as they attempt to follow through on their responsibilities:

- Failure in technology
- Current policies & procedures
- Disagreement/apposition from counterparts
- Budget/fiscal restraints
- Political climate may suggest other priorities are more important at the moment
- Competing calendars make it challenging to set appointments in a sooner timeframe.

Emerging leaders may need assistance when experiencing resistance. In the fitness world it is call spotting. Spotting is "the act of supporting another person during a particular exercise, with an emphasis on allowing the participant to lift or push more than they could normally do safely. Correct spotting involves knowing when to intervene and assist with a lift, and encouraging a training partner [mentee] to push beyond the point in which they would normally 'rack' the weight (return it to its stationary position." (https://en.wikipedia.org/wiki/Spotting_(weight_training))

Mentors should appropriately 'spot' their mentees as they incur greater than usual responsibility or resistance in the development process. This is most effective when mentors assist their mentees find immediate and real solutions to challenges faced in the execution of their responsibilities. For example, if technology failure is obstructing the mentee's progress, then providing access to adequate technology is imperative. In practice, this may require you to purchase new technology, exchange technology equipment amongst staff, or provide them access to your personal technology. Getting the proper stakeholders in the same room at the same time is often times a challenge as well. When competing calendars are preventing necessary meetings from occurring, you can "spot" your mentee by facilitating solutions. An online meeting, survey, or later than usual meeting time may be the answer. Whatever the case, simply put: help them SOLVE it.

The ultimate 'spotting' technique, what I consider the greatest benefit of the mentor-mentee relationship, is providing access to each other's sphere of influence, allowing for an expanded network of resources. Access to each other's sphere of influence compounds the relationship building process with more access points to assist with solving problems when they arise.

Developmental Impact to Self & Environment

Self-development occurs as the emerging leader learns to respond to challenges, perhaps by answering the following questions:

- How will executing the responsibility impact the environment?
- Does the reward of executing the responsibility outweigh the perceived challenges of execution?
- What skills are necessary to overcome the challenges?

These questions help the emerging leader learn about themselves, their counterparts, the environment and how to maneuver within the environment as they "observe and reflect on the experience, and create new approaches" (Kolb, 1985). Responses to the challenge further develops the leadership skills of the emerging leader, such as written and oral communication, computing, time management, inter-personal, delegation, synthesizing, and goal-setting, to name a few. Strategies to overcome these challenges are largely dependent on the time allotted to pursue solutions, the financial and human resources of the organization, and the attitude of the emerging leader.

The impact on the environment heavily relies on the emerging leader's ability to execute their responsibility with 1) effective communication and 2) completion within a designated timeframe as determined or needed by stakeholders and decision-makers. The following are examples of the types of outcomes emerging leaders may incur due to a lack of timely communication:

- No funding as a result of not submitting the request for funding by the request deadline.
- An unorganized meeting resulting from not having the meeting agenda or minutes completed by the start of the meeting.
- Poor attendance at an event due to not designing, printing, and distributing the marketing material.
- Delays of action or receipt of information as a result of not attending a meeting.

The ultimate impact for not engaging stakeholders and decision-makers with effective communication within the designated timeframe is a delayed or forfeited opportunity to successfully complete the task or make progress toward a specific goal that invariably impacts the environment. Knowing the consequences associated with poor or untimely execution should serve as a motivator against stagnation or procrastination.

Sustainable Outcome/Repetition

The sustainable outcome is reflected in the emerging leaders' attitude, behavior, and communication as they navigate the environment, manage time, effectively communicate, solve problems, and resolve conflict as they execute their responsibilities and build relationships with stakeholders and decision-makers. Continuous engagement or repetition with meaningful responsibilities, supported by the tenets of The Ellison Model, fosters sustainable outcomes that develop the leadership muscle and ultimately exemplary leadership.

Attitude: According to Hunt (2006b), "Attitude is an inspection station, which makes known the disposition of heart. It reveals where a person truly is in their community-building efforts. In short, 'attitude' is defined as alignment by leaders with ethical practices for inclusive community building or lack thereof." Mentors and mentees must demonstrate an aligned attitude of Honor, Respect, and Trust to inclusive community building.

Behavior: Hunt (2003) states "conflict is an imbalance between the conscience and the emotions. The conscience and the emotions are at war with the emotions bent on selfish gratification – one or the other will win." Accordingly, in the inclusive community building process, the behavior of the mentor and mentee must reflect an alignment of the conscience and the emotions that evidence care, share, and love for the community collective, unselfish traits, and integrity toward the environment.

Communication: According to Hunt (2007) article The ABCD's of Urban Renewal, "Communication relates to the message the mentor sends...If those in need of renewal feel the mentor is not serious about sound moral and ethical standards, he/she is not likely to produce the desired results." Affirming communication reflects words by the mentor and the mentee that support, strengthen and encourage respectful and honorable language regarding the collective, especially during times of resistance.

Discipline: At the Economic Empowerment Through Community Building Conference (2007) in Freeport, Bahamas, Dr. Michele Rice defined discipline as it related to The Ellison Model as "the self-restraint necessary to sustain one's self toward attitudes, behaviors, and factors of communication that facilitate the fostering of positive interpersonal and intra-personal relationships." Referencing again to Hunt's Theorem, discipline is both the mentor and mentee's ongoing display of a) inclusive community building attitudes, b) caring, sharing, and loving behaviors, and c) affirming communication, all of which are sustained and "nurtured" over time.

Within the Experiential Leadership Concept, mentors provide mentees a qualitative and quantitative experience. As the mentor grows proficiently in The Ellison Model tenets, so do their mentees. The following questions can help mentors and mentees reflect and critique their approach to mentoring and developing exemplary leadership:

- What attitude did you demonstrate while executing your responsibility?
- What challenges or resistance did you incur?
- What behaviors did you display when met with resistance?
- Did you use affirming communication or disparaging communication when met with resistance?
- What attitude, behaviors, and communications did you find helpful while going through the experiential process that you will continue to use as an approach in the future?

THE ELLISON MODEL AS A MANAGEMENT TOOL

Dudley Carter, my father, has been a managing supervisor for over 17 years in the maintenance and utilities department at various educational facilities including higher education. Dudley is also an entrepreneur. He and his business partner are a HVAC certified company that also carries a general contractors license. My father has often told me about his days as a farmer in Jamaica and the unsuspecting physical strength he possessed as a young boy. My father says he was stronger than an ox and used to kill lions with his bare hands. Some years ago my father had surgery on his rotator cuff, of which I reminded him that all the lion killing he did when growing up had caught up to him. He could not help but laugh. My father is a modest and meek man with an uncanny humor and wit. He's artful and masterful at using these jokes and other anecdotes from his farming days to make deep thought provoking points. He's not a complex man – the simplicity he possesses in understanding the world around us is as complex as he gets. He's ambidextrous: writes with his right hand and swings with his left. His golf stance and swing, for example, are unique to him, but he drives the ball over three hundred yards consistently.

Dudley has been trained on The Ellison Model from its inception. He is an excellent practitioner of the Model and carnivore of management practices and theories. He has developed excellent concepts about the approach to management, which he has both demonstrated and trained others on using. He specializes in the areas of customer service and professional development. Dudley fills the gaps offered by Total Quality Management (TQM), a popular customer service model from the 1980s that still drives the business approach of many companies today. Total Quality Management impacted the business world as companies shifted their focus from product services to people services. Fisher and Nair (2009) provide the following background on TQM:

> Explicit public focus on 'Quality Management' did not occur until the famous June 1980 NBC News report 'If Japan Can . . . Why Can't We?' that featured W. Edwards Deming, William Conway and reporter Lloyd Dobyns. However, the 1980 report created a watershed in the attention being paid by American companies to Quality Management. Quality Management consultants blossomed, companies started defining Quality in terms of Customers, and understanding and meeting customer needs became a major step towards business success...By the 1990s, it was not sufficient simply to 'meet customer needs': an increasingly competitive business environment meant that companies now had to deliver 'superior value' to customers. (p. 11)

Quality management and customer service are important elements of any successful business. With The Ellison Model to the forefront, certain gaps in

TQM become apparent, specifically, the disposition of heart of employees when engaging customers. Dudley expounds on this matter, citing the difference between what he calls customer service versus heart-felt service.

In the words of Dudley Carter
Customer Service Versus Heart-Felt Service

As owners of a small business, ICB Air Conditioning and Appliances, our top priority is service to our customers. As an organization, we practice The Ellison Model strategy for businesses. It is a character and economic business model that requires demonstration and it is what sets us apart from other companies. We operate our business according to the tenets of The Ellison Model. Some of these tenets are respect, trust, honor, and transparency. These are characteristics of those who truly have the interest of the customer at heart. We are not just trying to sell something to the customer, but rather sell the customer what he or she needs. This is part of definition of "heart felt service." The customer service staff of many businesses is commonly taught to greet their customers with a smile, and address them personally. While these are desirable attributes that anyone would expect from someone who is providing them with service, the question is, are those traits genuine? If it is not genuine, but simply learned behavior, it can be labeled as customer service. When the service is not sincere, the person's motive is questionable.

The Ellison Model teaches us to see our customer from the perspective of the heart. The heart is the innermost part of a person, and when the motive of the heart is one of love, then the service is genuine and sincere. When we engage in heart-felt service we are willing to be patient, caring and honest with our customers. When one engages in heart- felt service, that one sees his customers as stakeholders in the business. The customers are viewed as partners from this perspective. Partners that help the business become more successful. If the partners (customers) are helping the success of the business, then it is only fair that we aim to be as helpful and honest as possible. Our goal is to service our clients by way of the tenets and values of The Ellison Model. Our desire is that as our clients experience satisfaction with our attitude and performance that they too will see the value and importance in adopting The Ellison Model as their own.

In the words of Dudley Carter
Preparing Staff For Work

The top down approach to supervision has never seemed to work well. Work is often times just not fun for many in the workforce. They sometimes see themselves as slaves to work with somebody always telling them what to do, how fast to get the work done, and when to get the work done. Supervisors are sometimes viewed as slave drivers.

My employees told me they had to drag themselves out of bed to come to work. As a supervisor of the university housing department, I realized that it was necessary to possess the skill to know how to lead my staff into getting things done. It was a situation where everyone had to be on one accord because students, facility, and staff, including the directors, were depending on my staff and I to keep the facility clean and safe. The question that the Ellison Model asked was, where is the care, share, love, trust, respect and honor? Where is the approach of inclusiveness? As the Model taught me those principles, I realized that first I had to be the Model. I then became as one that was like the inner-circle of a clock, seeing my staff on the outside. I then realized how important it was to pull my staff into that inner-circle with me. The model taught me to "flip the script." This was a simple concept. Instead of preparing work for my staff, why not prepare my staff for the work? In this way the emphasis was not placed solely on work but more so on my staff, where they are empowered to effectively manage the workload and not let the workload manage them.

I began to see my staff beyond just being staff. Their names were not staff. Their names were Mary, Jose', Marie, Daniel, etc., who got the work done. These were real people. With this in mind, The Ellison Model became synonymous to a Ferris wheel, in which everyone gets the opportunity to ride together and take turn being at the top. The Ferris wheel doesn't see color, race, nationality or gender. That Wheel is a Teacher, showing me that I am not the only supervisor, but as the Wheel spins, and puts me at the bottom, it is time for me to see who is on top. And though I am a supervisor, the individual at the top becomes a mentor to me. In these instances my staff is able to help prepare me for work also. In this concept, I could see what a true mentor-mentee relationship is about. I did not say we did not have other challenges, but as we continued to ride the Ferris wheel, we learned that "it's not the problem that counts, it's the solution."

Dudley Carter's Ferris wheel concept corroborates the **leader-follower exchange** discussed in chapter four, which states that success in a group setting is achieved when all parties allow space for leading and following as deemed appropriate. No matter how you splice any of its components in any sector of society, the fact that people run the world, will always make every matter an issue of personnel. Therefore, by embracing the principles of The Ellison Model, additional creative ideas that plug in concepts to further inclusion, multicultural appreciation, conflict resolution, mentorship, and relationship building becomes a fluid part of your growth and development as an emerging leader. As mentioned before, The Ellison Model maintains the wholeness of its sum in its parts. As stated by Dudley, the professional development goal of preparing staff for work and promoting heart-felt service matures employees into being the right employee in the right place at the right time – with a continuous goal that over time, the rightness of employee is displayed all the time. These beautiful and poignant concepts on heart-felt service, staff development, and the Ferris wheel/leader-follower exchange presented by Dudley Carter are practical to adopt.

Reflective Journal Moment

13. As a mentor, advisor, or supervising manager, in what ways have your provided development opportunities for your staff/mentees that included meaningful responsibilities, challenges/resistance, impact, and sustainable outcomes?

14. Do you prepare work for staff or staff for work? Elaborate on your answer.

15. How do you ensure that everyone on your team is deemed a leader in the Ferris wheel/leader-follower exchange approach?

PRAXIS:

A LOOK AT

THE ELLISON

MODEL IN

PLAY

Chapter 7

"Give me but a firm spot on which to stand, and I shall move the earth." – Archimedes, The Works of Archimedes

The multi-dimensional platform, adoptive possibilities, and fluidity of The Ellison Model provide a robust, yet simple approach to character and leadership development. By allowing the model to guide your motivation, attitude, and behaviors toward self, mentorship, and the collective community, solutions to how individuals and groups engage each other to create alignment in their pursuit of progress becomes a sustainable "way of life." The cumulative components of the model provide leaders a turnkey rubric to assess their intrinsic values and outward expressions of building inclusive community. Leaders develop solutions using The Ellison Model by allowing The Ellison Model to develop, mentor, and lead them.

The Ellison Model technique *Community Moment-Teachable Second-Sustainable Teachable Second* is a three-part process that guides us from a thought provoking or life changing experience, to the sharing of that experience, to presenting the experience in a sustainable format. A *community moment* is similar to having an "aha" moment, a moment of clarity, or understanding of a particular experience that creates growth in the individual. A *teachable second* occurs when we share the community moment with another individual. In sharing, other individuals are able to learn the lesson without having had the direct experience. A *Sustainable Teachable Second* occurs when the community moment is shared in a format usually considered as long lasting. A sustainable format may include a book, song, movie, short film, podcast, or a live stream program that allows individuals to reference the material and capture the experience at their leisure.

The following community moments are from individuals who have implemented The Ellison Model in their professional, academic, and personal lives. Each example shows a practical way of implementing the Model on a long-term basis, in addition to solving an internal or external conflict. The community moments also reveal epiphanies and new methodologies tried and tested as individuals allowed the Model to curate their disposition of heart, making them the right person in the right place at the right.

Story #1: Seasoned Educator Karen Lundy Withstands And Stands In The Public Education System

If a person speaks to a current educator there is a high probability that he or she could give a laundry list of issues being faced in the classroom and beyond regarding students, administration, public policies and funding. As an educator, The Ellison Model has provided me with the strength and stamina to continue in the profession of educating students despite the issues that seem so apparent.

Just this year I recall one of my students having a seeming blockage in learning and recalling basic math concepts, even with the constant repetition and practice provided in class and encouragement to do so at home. I worked with this student one on one, using manipulatives, all while speaking encouraging words to him. I was hoping that the epiphany would come and he would not only understand, but also be able to explain to others how to solve the types of multiplication word problems we were studying. Just before the winter break, the insight came.

> *"This is a sustainable work and he will remember!"*

Previously I had gone to his first grade teacher to inquire about whether he struggled with math. She confirmed he did and also in processing in reading. His second grade teacher began the intervention process that teachers are required to do when students demonstrate deficiencies. So when this student mastered the process of problem solving in multiplication, I was thrilled and shared this with his first grade teacher. Her response was, "Don't worry, he'll forget it by next week!" My immediate response was one that would not allow her negative words to impact this child. I responded, "No, this is a sustainable work and he will remember!" She shrugged in a nonchalant manner and walked away.

With the approaching two-week break from school, many teachers began to speak about all that the students will forget and the loss of learning that will occur. I kept positive thoughts as The Ellison Model espouses. After winter break, yes, the student returned and nothing was lost – his learning was sustained even through the two-week winter recess.

This was a testament to me of the working of The Ellison Model values of caring, sharing and loving—caring enough to ignore the negative thoughts, sharing those things that I have and loving my students enough to unselfishly give that which I have that would benefit them. Initially, I was concerned about this student, given the high number of African American boys being staffed into special education classes. To see this type of sustainable breakthrough in math was wonderful not just for me, but for the student himself, who continued to make strides in both reading and math.

Story #2: Financial Analyst Alfredo Alderete Sees the Bigger Picture of Inclusion Across Many Industries

As a child I learned that I was not a poor or rich person, but my family was a low-income earners. My father used to take us on tours visiting churches. He gave my brothers and I used shoes and clothes that were donated by generous people. It was around that time that I started thinking of how society was organized. I thought then that there were people who give and those who received, and I did not like to be at that end of the equation. I promised that I would be one who gives when I grow up.

"It was there that I understood that there is another group in society besides those who give and take. The third group is the Collaborators."

I held that belief for years until I was introduced to The Ellison Model. I was taking a course with Mr. Carter while I was dealing with my job, other careers, and applying for scholarships. It was in the middle of this mess that I started understanding the powerful concept of The Ellison Model. It was there that I understood that there is another group in society besides those who give and take. The third group is the Collaborators. This group is the one that make great things happen by creating organizations that allows the participation of many (inclusion).

For instance in a free market like the U.S. one might think that cutthroat competition is the key to success. Yet we have many examples of large companies that were able to create value by creating partnerships and collaboration. For example, RED Hat, a Linux open source software was created by the collaboration of thousands of developers. The Apple app platform is open to anyone who wants to create an app. The Apple environment of inclusion, or what I call collaboration, has created more than a million apps.

Another phenomenon that has taken is what is called the "shared economy." Companies like Uber created a platform where people who own a car can offer a car service during their down time. AirBnB offers the same kind of platform for rooms. Anybody who has an available room for a day or months can rent it to the open market. These shared economies are disrupting old rigid systems. Taxicabs in large cities have created a high barrier to enter through the years. A license to operate a taxicab in New York City can go for around $1000. Now with Uber those barriers are gone.

For me, I am still experiencing the power of collaboration. I designed a solution to lower the cost of collecting evidence to be used in legal defense cases. I saw a problem in the legal system and I took action to solve it. My project is still in the development phase (at the point of writing this), but so far I can tell you the challenges that I had getting started.

I had an idea but I did not have a clue on how to bring it to life. My first contact was a professor who teaches social entrepreneurship. He collaborated with me over lunch to design possible business models to bring this idea to life. Next, I needed developers to help me build the platform that is needed to integrate some of the legal stakeholders on managing evidence. I was fortunate enough to meet an IT-Security banker from one of the largest banks in the world. He sat with me and helped me understand the components and structure I needed to make this project secure. Also, I met two people online from Venezuela that were willing to collaborate on this project. For them the lack of transparency in the collection of evidence was a daily issue in their country. They worked endless hours to develop the basics of the project to be able to participate in a competition in New York for new tech ideas.

Today, I have more than 14 people collaborating in making this project possible. It is not done yet. But the point here is that even though I had the idea of a solution, it was not enough to make this concept a reality. As I write, I have very professional and passionate people collaborating with their best skills to bring this project a life. What would be the consequence of bringing this project alive? We are going to build better communities by allowing the people to have better chances of defending themselves in cases of arrest.

Story #3: The Unknown Bias: Nicole Parris-Brown Opens Up About Her Closed-Off World

When it came to sharing of myself with certain persons, I realized there was a bias in me. This bias or prejudice played out based on personal beliefs and socialization from family, and I dare say church. I realized one day, when asked about my friends and whom I spent time with, I only associated with persons with the same or a similar Caribbean background.

I am a descendent of Bahamian ancestry and culture and took great pride in it. Having a family that was diligent about keeping up with our family history rooting back to Zaire, brought to the Bahamas as slaves, and how we are here today was monumental. My family has always taken pride in hard work and the many obstacles overcome by the elders so that we can have greater opportunities to be successful. While growing up, there were always messages of being pro-black, so a Caucasian as a mate was not approved. I remember as a child asking, "What if I wanted to date and marry a white guy?" The response was, "You can't bring him here!" There were also messages about Black Americans who were lazy and shouldn't have handouts because they did not work towards success. I was also told that Black Americans, although they had some of the same opportunities to become independent in life, would rather depend on others and the government for daily needs and avoid jobs to maintain the assistance. These were major influences on my outlook of people in life.

> "I was a product of my environment — exclusive in my friendships, mates, and outlook on people. It became clear I was not as inclusive as I thought."

As a young adult who had managed to successfully earn a high school education and working on the bachelor's degree, I was a product of my environment – exclusive in my friendships, mates, and outlook on people. It became clear I was not as inclusive as I thought. I too had devalued some Black Americans and Caucasians in a similar manner to how people of color were treated in slavery. Although I was a practicing Christian, I quickly saw there was some hypocrisy in my way of life. I did not love, care about and share with everyone, nor did I truly honor, trust and respect all people. If you were not in my circle meeting certain unwritten criteria, then you were not

for everyone

given a chance to share and exchange values. The ironic thing is by the law of the land I am considered a Black woman but did not share the same sentiments as other Black Americans due to the negative perception I was made to believe.

By working in the Multicultural Program and Services office, I first had to overcome the conflict within me of being prejudice and seeing my American colleagues and myself, not based on heritage, but rather, just people who were just like me. These were people who wanted a better life and were working to be successful. In order for us to truly be a team and promote TEM as a way of life, I had to become the TEM model. I learned to give others a fair chance to be a part of the community, our community. I also learned, as it related to other ethnicities, to not exclude based on color – they are people too.

Story #4: CPA David Ritchey Cashes in on the Opportunity to Teach Budgeting and Community Building

I've worked in public accounting for over ten years. During that time, I've gained much knowledge and experience in the areas of accounting for various entities, tax preparation, business consulting, managerial accounting, financial reporting, and auditing. These are highly specialized areas.

After spending over ten years in public accounting, I accepted a position working for Miami Dade County, one of the largest county government in the United States of America. I held high-level positions within the County government, all within the Enterprise Fund Departments. An enterprise fund is a department that operates as a self-sustaining business and does not rely on tax dollars. The departments that I held positions in include Financial Reporting and Cost Accounting Manager for Miami Dade Solid Waste; Capital Finance Administrator for the Aviation Department; Controller for Miami Dade Seaport Department; Assistant Director of Finance and Budgeting for Miami Dade Transit Department; and Assistant Director of Contract Compliance and Performance Improvement for Miami Dade County Water and Sewer Department.

With all my training and professional experience, I could only develop staff in various areas from a technical standpoint. However, I was not able to teach or train in a manner that was truly sustainable and transferable to every walk of life until I was trained in and incorporated The Ellison Model. As a result, I have incorporated the GOMABCD seven-step process at my work place in meetings, speaking engagements, and professional trainings. There have been much buy-in and agreement, even to the point that certain people are calling themselves GOMA.

> *"Your caring, loving and honest approach built trust with the believers and they were willing to accept the wealth of information you provided."*

Because of my professional background, I was asked if I would train the Board of Directors (The Board) of Clara Mohammed School of South Florida on the proper way to establish a budget and account for the schools' activity. Clara Mohammed School is a Muslim-based organization founded in 1967. I knew this training had to be extremely effective because it would impact many people, including the students who attend the school. Thus, the approach to budgeting and accounting had to first be GOMA-fied using an TEM technique.

The Goal, Objective, Method, and Attitude of the Board had to be made right. They all needed to be operating on the same page. That is, they must agree with GOMA. The primary focus was on the Board, teaching them about attitude, behavior, communication, and discipline as it relates to being board members who oversees the functions and activities while establishing policies and procedures of a school. A few of the members wanted to know when was I going to start teaching them about budgeting? I told them that I am teaching budget as we speak. Just as you would when you approach "Conflict Resolution", you first examine one's self before looking outside at others. Likewise, when working as a board, you examine yourself to see if you are operating from the right GOMA perspective.

After the true budgeting process was GOMA-fied the Board was prepared to receive the standard/normal method of how to prepare a budget. The Board perfectly received this training. It is evident by the follow up email received from the Board Chairperson Ms. Patricia Z. Salahuddin. She wrote the following remarks regarding the training: *"Thank you for helping us to GOMA-fy our budget. Your method of showing and involving us made a world of difference in our perspective of budgeting. Your caring, loving and honest approach built trust with the believers and they were willing to accept the wealth of information you provided. May God continue to bless you in your efforts and may He continue to guide you as you share your knowledge to make this world a better place for His servants."*

Story #5: Tom Ellison Discovers the Correction Needed for Himself and Inmates in the Florida Prison System

I began my career in government service with the Illinois Department of Corrections. After 18 years in Illinois, I was employed by the Florida Department of Corrections at a female correctional facility. I was responsible for the release of inmates who had to have physicals prior to release, in addition to addressing their needed medications, and/or arrangement for any post release treatment. I did not know anything about the Ellison Model or conflict resolution, for that matter, upon coming to this new position. All I knew was there was a need to communicate with all the departments of the institution, including the medical personnel

> *"My frustrations with the system were as much my own as I was part of that circle of diversity, dis-unity, and dis-community."*

responsible for scheduling the medical needs of inmates pending release. I knew it would take all parties working together to get the job done.

I had two basic rules that I talked about, "No Violence or Threats Of Violence" which applied to both staff and inmates in all circumstances. Later on, I came to understand by way of TEM that situations would require more than that, as the intra-institutional conflicts would often arise when someone dropped the ball. For example, when the day of release came, I found out that a medical issue had not been addressed. Higher-ups would inquire, "Why is this inmate still here?" Upon giving the answer, fingers were usually pointed to the medical department or myself – sometime to the both of us. I later learned that at times a physician was not available to conduct the physical exam.

My initial thinking was that the employees were supposed to be in charge of the all aspects of the institution involving employees, inmates, and visitors. What I found out was that these areas were all points of division. When blame time came, Classification Department would assign blame to Medical; Medical would blame Security; and Security would blame Classification.

As I was introduced to The Ellison Model, it touched on the need for relationship building in order to get the task accomplished. As best as I was able to understand TEM I tried to employ it on the job. Unfortunately, the resistance turned its focus on me as the odd man out. It occurred to me that I had to demonstrate TEM in the way I behaved. For example, when having lunch, and talk began about who dropped the ball, I would remind them that the day would come when it be your turn to be blamed because the divisive forces were no respecter of persons. I found out that I could not turn anyone from established institutional practices as they were fixed in the minds of those who were there before me. They would tell me that from time to time, the problem was that I thought I knew a thing or two also.

The Ellison Model showed me that I did not know enough to deal with all aspects of the problems. I wish I could say I solved every conflict that I encountered. The Model taught me that Conflict was "Unitary Process" where each person had to learn how to acknowledge and deal with their part in the situation. My frustrations with the system were as much my own as I was part of that circle of diversity, dis-unity, and dis-community. The Model caused me to come to the knowledge that I had to move from that diversity, to unity, to community to be effective in resolving my part in the conflict.

Story #6: Heart-felt Service from Chef Crystal a "Qui" Harvey Was The Right Attitude Needed for This Brewing Conflict

As part of my weekly duties to provide lunch for a private inner city school, I quickly came to an understating that one size might not fit all when it comes to feeding children. A few weeks ago, my colleague and I received a call from the school stating the children were not happy with the meal items prepared. Having entered into this contract midway through the year, we were a little different from the previous catering company. When feeding a school that seeks reimbursement from the government, there are rules that must be followed. Primarily, the school must follow certain healthy eating guidelines. Chiefly, all grains must be whole grains, and vegetables and fruits are a focal point of the menu, as well as milk must be 1% or low-fat. The aforementioned items were different from what the children had grown accustomed.

After receiving a call from the client pertaining to their meal, I realized how important possibly how problematic this situation was going. The call was from an apparently perturbed staff member who very sternly stated, "Many of the children are not eating the food." When she was done with the conversation, she attempted to hang up the phone, but somehow the call remained active. She could be heard cursing out of frustration and saying the food ordered was a waste of the school's money. Eventually, the call was disconnected and that is when I had to consider the situation myself. This process of following the strict guidelines of the state, and also trying to keep in mind the likes and dislikes of the students tried to frustrate me. After speaking to my colleague about the situation, we agreed that we would try a different approach. We wanted to maintain a good business relationship with the school; we wanted the kids to eat so they could be nourished; we wanted to comply with state regulations; and we wanted harmony.

> *"After visiting the school and speaking to her in a non-combative way, we were able to avoid any further negative criticism."*

Ah-ha! It came to us to speak to the staff and get a better understanding of what the children preferred to eat. With this in mind, we'd have to be creative in including the healthy stuff to ensure sustenance. But, in order to solve the issue this meant addressing the unhappy and disgruntled staff member.

After visiting the school and speaking to her in a non-combative way, we were able to avoid any further negative criticism. After a few laughs, we found out the cause of her concern was she did not like to see the food thrown away. Turns out she really had the children's interest in mind. We came to an understanding that the relationship building focus of The Ellison Model was an outcome of an attitude of excellence pertaining to feeding the children. Subsequently, were able to put together a menu more to the liking of the kids and school representative.

Story #7: How Do You Go From a "C" to an "A" School? Principal Richard Garrick Knew The Principles Of Goma Could

As the principal of Lauderhill Paul Turner Elementary School in Lauderhill, FL, I was able to implement the School Afterschool Program. As a part of the program, all students, faculty, staff, and volunteers had to undergo the GOMA Educator Training. It was my hope that the training would have a positive impact on their lives and also be a benefit to the larger community of Lauderhill Paul Turner Elementary School.

The goal of the School Afterschool Program was to develop a cadre of faculty and staff who are equipped, prepared, and engaged as *inclusive community builders* by way of The Ellison Model for the uplifting and unification of the Community (students, staff, parents and partners).

The objectives were to establish a School After School program focused on immersing students in a culture that fosters character development and that teaches them the fundamentals of economic development via entrepreneurship; provide each participant with tools to recognize their internal mentoring voice and to guide them to overcome all challenges (social, emotional, educational, etc.); and unify attendees as members of the inclusive community as persistent, conscientious, and disciplined learners and dispensers of knowledge.

The methods that we utilized were that teachers and all stakeholders would give maximum effort in their educational practices to encourage academic and school excellence throughout the school community.

Identifying, contacting, and working with strategic partners, (i.e. School Advisory Council, Children's Services Council of Broward County) and other agencies that are willing to support this School After School program. Teachers and all stakeholders will receive professional development in The GOMA Educator training.

In order to bring these matters forth, it was necessary for all participants (faculty, staff and students) to have the right attitude where they learned how to work in a caring, sharing, loving and inclusive environment in which they demonstrated trust, honor and respect for themselves and others.

Students may obtain knowledge and skills, but are often found lacking in matters of citizenship, civility, and brotherhood/sisterhood. The School After

for everyone

School program inculcates students in values that foster inclusive community building. The program is designed as noncompetitive to traditional schooling, but rather as a Gap Learning approach. In the School After School program setting, students learned how to "put on" and employ The Ellison Model lens of inclusion in governing their personal and interpersonal relations, and analyzing behavior whether in real life or in the curricular text.

As a result of all of the Lauderhill Paul Turner stakeholders and students buying into the GOMA curriculum via the School Afterschool Program, we have seen the positive things learned evidenced by an increase in positive student behavior, teacher efficacy and student engagement to name a few of the benefits. We were able to "Gomafy" Lauderhill Paul Turner by turning negative situations to positive ones using the GOMABCD 7 Step Process.

Story #8: Line Service Technician Lawrence Darville Decides 'Tit-for-Tat' is Not Where It's At

The time spent as a Line service tech requires that aircrafts be fueled, moved from one location of the airport to another, and serviced. In addition, deboarding passenger needs are to be met, whether it was having their vehicles staged upon arrival to providing assistance with bags. During months of peak season, the workload would double and could be quite exhausting when absent adequate manpower. During these busy times, our supervisor would often be seen sitting in the office while others worked tirelessly. During these instances, the shift would be understaffed requiring a greater effort from all persons present to execute their tasks effectively. Numerous employees took issue with this as well as myself and would voice it amongst us. We agreed that it was very selfish of our supervisor to sit while we worked. We also agreed how things could have been more efficiently had he assisted.

> *"At this instance it dawned on me that this "tit for tat" attitude was not helping..."*

The problem was that our supervisor still did not help despite word getting back to him – he did not seem to care. This diminished the morale of the current workers tremendously as some felt and expressed that if the supervisor was not going to pull his weight and simply do the bare minimum, so would they.

At this instance it dawned on me that this "tit for tat" attitude was not helping because some passengers had to handle their own bags, and often times tasks were delayed or simply went undone because of the overall response of those present. This was not good for business. It came to me that if we took the same approach that our supervisor did regarding work that things would only get worse as the workload would continue to pile up.

The approach given to me was to work in a manner that we wanted our supervisor to work. In other words, my attitude had to be one such that I stopped comparing what my supervisor did to the work ethic I had. I also had to change my behavior to that of someone who was going to do his part and possibly my supervisor's part if need be. My communication was such that it had to move from complaining about Jo my supervisor to not complaining at all. My discipline was such that whether or not my supervisor worked, I would.

After some time had passed and as others saw that various one's attitudes toward the supervisor had changed, there were little complaints about what wasn't being done to what was being done. Soon after, our supervisor John could be seen outside with the remainder of the workers on the shift assisting as we all desired.

Story #9: Charge Nurse Aida Munroe Audits the Heart of Her Department at Work

In preparing for this years' audit season, we had a mock run during the latter part of last year. There were some lessons that had to be learned. In that, we had a staff meeting to assess what went wrong and what was done right. I expressed the GOMABCD method way of doing things as I did in a previous meeting with another Insurance company. Peter was the lead auditor. He was a very bright young man. He approached me after the meeting and asked, "Can we meet and you show me the methods that you used?" I agreed, we met, and he was in full agreement with the model.

In future meetings I would hear Peter talking about Goal, Objective, Method and Attitude. Later when we gathered to implement The Model through training and program design, my immediate supervisor said, "Remember we are one Molina!" I knew then that there was total agreement. At the time I was a temporary employee, and was only contracted to be there from October to November 30, 2016. They kept extending the contract, and eventually asked me to come on permanently.

Peter was also promoted to Manager of the entire department. Our department, unlike in the past, now meets our quota and auditing requirements. We've even been in the 2nd position compared to other departments.

Story #10: The Power of a Positive Attitude Provided the Right Kind of Negative Results for Cancer Free Francina Hosea

My name is Francina Hosea. I work for a nursing and rehabilitation facility in the administration department. In October (which happens to be breast awareness month) I had my first mammogram. A couple of months later I went to a scheduled doctor's visit only to find out from his nurse practitioner that my results were irregular. She was very brief and she did not examine me. There was something truly going on with her. She seemed fatigued and unpleasant. The nurse assisting even asked if she was leaving her at the office. I was wondering why didn't they call me in sooner and what is going on with me.

Sometime later that week I made an appointment to have my ultrasound and CT scan done. The nurse practitioner I mentioned earlier had written prescriptions for me to have both. While at the diagnostic center I was told that I could have my CT done but not my ultrasound. Somehow in the midst of the nurse practitioner not being herself she forgot to write if it was the right or left breast. Not only so they could take the right exam but for insurance purposes also. I ended up leaving without the exam and following up with my doctor who was able to correct the script. That was not the only news. Upon him reading the report he realized that the exam did not call for the right or the left but bilateral. I ended up traveling from the diagnostic center, to the doctor, and back to the breast center spending countless hours and hundreds of dollars.

My mother joined me on my doctor visits as I went back and forth. For every appointment, biopsy incision, and session my mother and I fellowshipped, encouraged the other people in the waiting room and the doctors and nurses; we even prayed with some of the other patients.

Not knowing the results of such a test, my attitude remained extremely positive for others and myself in the facility. My attitude allowed me to engage others and be positive in my interaction for their benefit. It turned out that my test results showed, and indeed I Am, cancer free.

Story #11: Operations Supervisor of Sanitation Derrick Lundy Sr. Learns Pride Is The Real Trash To Dump

I have been a government employee as an operations supervisor with the City of Miami Beach for ten years. I have served as a mid- level manager that oversees the operation within the Public Works Department. I came to the city with much experience from the business sector and upon my arrival I thought I had much to add to this city. Their management skills dealing with conflicts and managing resources was in need of a lot of help. It became apparent very quickly that the entire team managed by the seat of their pants in every situation. Well, you can imagine the culture shock that I experienced coming from the business sector, where it is very structured and money is the name of the game.

With that being said, it was definitely a learning experience coming to the City of Miami Beach because saving money or being efficient did not appear to be a top priority. I immediately saw the need for The Ellison Model and I did my best to implement all what I knew about TEM. In the beginning it seemed to have an impact that was promising. However, because it was inclusive and required the sharing of resources, it seemed to bring about opposition from those that were in charge. What I did not fully understand was why the cliques that made up the division would not allow the coming together. I figured it was probably because of fear of losing power or status within the organization.

Indeed frustration and anger began to settle in me and I found myself hating the people I was supposed to be serving. Well years passed and it took just that long for me to realize that within me the conflict had to be corrected first and then I could help those who were also conflicted to make that transition. Pride had set in and I was not aware of it. I did not have the right attitude in me. I was in need of TEM first and then I could show others what exactly TEM is by way of my behavior. So in a sense, Miami Beach taught me even the more about TEM than what I was expecting to teach Miami Beach about TEM.

Story #12: ICB Productions Manager Dexter Hunt Runs From Racism To the Man in the Mirror

Having grown up as an African American male I faced a lot of racism. Some of which was overt and other times subtle. An example of the overt is one day I was walking down the street in my neighborhood and a truck drove from the right lane into the left lane (as I was walking in the opposite direction of the truck) directly in front of me. I literally dove into someone's yard to avoid collision. As the truck roared by me, the driver yelled "Go home nigger" while violently gesturing his fist toward me. There was another time in college when someone defaced my automobile with racial slurs while I was in class. There were the many times that after playing with a group of friends, upon returning to one of their houses for a snack that I was the only one not allowed in the house because the parent said that I was "dirty". Such situations began to cause me to develop a hatred for Caucasian people. I was reared in a predominately African American environment (neighbors, schools etc.) This rearing short sided my perspective even more as the few times that I had to deal with others races many times ended with some sort of prejudicial outcome.

Sometime during my second year of college I was riding in car with my roommate (who was also African America and shared many of the same views that I did) when we made a stop at a red light. A car with two Caucasian males pulled up beside us. I made eye contact with the driver of the car and he smiled and spoke to me. I grunted something back as the light turn green and we pulled off. My rhetorical question to my roommate was "Why do you think they spoke to us?" I had already concluded (based upon my life experience with Caucasians that there was some devious motive behind him speaking to me.

Later, as I reflected on the situation, my training in The Ellison Model kicked in. I realized that I was in a state of conflict. The Ellison Model or TEM teaches that during a situation of conflict that the issue (or points of conflict) must be resolved in oneself first. Even if the other guy had some deep seeded devious motive, it was incumbent on me to take the first step and resolve this issue with myself before I could even consider addressing someone else. By doing as TEM dictates, I was able to release myself from the position of conflict. It allowed me to see the situation clearer, to view the issue with wider parameters, and to make an honest assessment of the situation. TEM got me to point the finger at myself first, only realize that thing that I was accusing others of; I was actually doing to them. My perspective on life had a positive change after applying TEM's conflict resolution principles. Because of TEM 's directives, I changed my perspective on not only Caucasians but also other races, organizations, genders and more.

Story #13: The Ellison Model Project – Alfonso Ritchey

In 2005 I began working on Miami Beach as an Operational Supervisor for the Sanitation Division. I had been a supervisor for a private company for a long period of time before this new assignment and had many years of experience in this industry. My take on the job and the employees was that I had seen every situation before and there probably wouldn't be an instance where I hadn't been successful in. I then began to have issues with the employees and found myself being frustrated with things that should have been simple fixes. I had developed an attitude of discommunity towards the job and the workers because I thought myself to be above whatever came to me. I was seemingly more educated and was given a higher position than others who desired the position. In my thoughts, I was steeped

> *"I had developed an attitude of discommunity towards the job and the workers because I thought myself to be above whatever came to me."*

in discommunity because I did not see the attitude of inclusion to be valuable to me. I faced a real challenge for some time until I saw the impact of my attitude as being one that separated me from others. I saw myself as having the only value around me, so that which others could contribute to my experience was lost.

Once I saw the destructive attitude for what it was I began to see things very differently. I saw that it took inclusion to be successful on any job. I could then see how valuable my co-workers were because though they may not have been the most formally educated they brought the experience of working for a municipality to the table, and that is what I did not have. As I appreciated their experience, I could offer my feedback; the flow of their experience opened up to me even more than before. They later grew to see me as one that they needed to protect because the lines of information flowed both ways. The more I saw that I needed the employees' information and resources as much as they needed mine, I could see the need for caring, sharing, and loving to go on in all of my life experiences. The Ellison Model foci that I would say summed up my experience is relationship building. I learned to value the input and resources of others.

Story #14: The Ellison Model Testimony; Increasing Inventory Turns From Jameel Barnes

In 2010 I worked at Hospital Corporation of America (HCA), as the Division Pharmacy Inventory Procurement Analyst. I was responsible for training and developing the 13 Pharmacy Buyers in our Division. Our corporate office tasked me with increasing the inventory turns for our division. Inventory turns are the number of times inventory is sold or used in a specific time period.

I was charged to make sure our 13 Buyers had inventory turns of 10 or higher. When I first began at HCA I supervised the Buyers, as they did monthly cycle counts (an inventory auditing procedure that helps manage inventory). After a couple of years of performing these cycle counts our CEO, Division Pharmacy Director of Operations and I decided to stop doing cycle counts. We decided the outcome of the cycle counts was not worth the time and resources used. The Buyers were elated when I told them they no longer had to do cycle counts.

When the corporate office issued the charge of getting every pharmacy up to 10 inventory turns or higher our CEO and Directors wanted me to go back to making the Buyers do monthly cycle counts. I reminded them why we had stopped doing the cycle counts and insured them that we would reach the inventory turn goal by the end of the year.

I assumed the role of the mentor and my Pharmacy Buyers were the mentees. I conducted weekly Buyer's Calls and taught them The Ellison Model. I proceeded to teach the Buyers the fundamental principles of inventory management. They needed that knowledge in order understand the goal of reaching an inventory turn of 10 or higher. I gave them measurable objectives to reach on a weekly and monthly basis. They understood that these objectives lead them toward reaching the inventory turn goal. The method we used was outlined and detailed. The weekly calls were used to collect feedback and share opportunities to improve our methods/processes. The weekly calls also served as a vehicle to keep communication flowing. I made it clear to the Buyers that a positive attitude of inclusion was critical to us reaching this goal.

The Ellison Model, via GOMA, made reaching the inventory turn goal so much easier than doing monthly cycle counts. The buyer learned a lot about inventory management from me and I learned a lot about pharmaceuticals from them. Strong relationships were built, which assisted in future projects.

Story #15: Who is "The Model"? Esquire Deryl G. Hunt, II Honors His Father and Ellison Model Creator

> "I too, am The Ellison Model."

The impactful experience that I have had with The Ellison Model that I wish to share comes before "The Ellison Model" was named as such. It comes from my interaction with the author of the model, Dr. Deryl G Hunt, over the past 30+ years. Over more than 30 years, Dr. Hunt has exhibited the values that underlie the model and has taught many individuals about the value of caring, sharing, loving, trust, honor, and respect.

I witnessed the development of The Model from Dr. Hunt's early days at Florida international University. I saw the techniques being formulated, the values being established, and diagrams developed. I saw the impact that The Ellison Model had on individuals far and wide as they adopted the tenets as their own. I saw Dr. Helen Ellison, the namesake of the model, delight in championing The Model because she realized how impactful it was. With all of these positive things occurring, it did not yet occur to me the true nature of The Model.

The moment of epiphany came when I realized a simple truth: that Dr. Hunt is The Ellison Model and that all along he had been teaching us to likewise be The Ellison Model. The Model, at its core stresses mentorship -- molding mentees in the image of the mentor. This is what Dr. Hunt did – he befriended Dr. Helen Ellison and taught her a new inclusive way of life, so much so that toward the end of her natural life, she had begun to mentor others in like manner as inclusive community builders.

We can learn from the model of Dr. Helen Ellison that inclusion is not innate – it must be learned from a teacher steeped in its core values. I learned that The Ellison Model is more than charts, texts, or set of values. It is a way of life animated by the spirit of unity ensuring that an individual is part of the inclusive community of the like-minded. In full disclosure, Dr. Hunt is also my father and we share the same name. Yet, he is more than a father to me. He is a mentor who has modeled The Ellison Model and has taught me that I too, am The Ellison Model.

Reflective Journal Moment

16. How has The Ellison Model worked to improve your goal, objective, method, attitude, behavior, communication, and discipline?

THE
FINAL
SAY

Chapter 8

The Seven Social Sins are: "Wealth without work. Pleasure without conscience. Knowledge without character. Commerce without morality. Science without humanity. Worship without sacrifice. Politics without principle."—From a sermon given by Frederick Lewis Donaldson in Westminster Abbey, London, on March 20, 1925.

O ver the decades Hunt and his associates, myself included, have used the performing, visual, and musical arts to creativity communicate and capture the tenets of caring, sharing, loving, trust, honor, and respect. A handful of full production plays, skits, and more than 100 songs have been written as theme music, soundtracks, and meditative composition to encourage inclusive community building. There is a certain type of poetry to it all. The Community Anthem Song and the poem Article of Character are two such pieces of dramatic work that stand out as sustainable teaching seconds.

Community Anthem Song

The Star Spangled Banner, written by Francis Scott Key, has not always been accepted as the anthem for ALL Americans, specifically Black Americans who recognize the sting of an enslaved past. However, many Blacks since 1900 have regarded *Life Every Voice and Sing*, written by James Weldon Johnson and his brother J. Rosamond, as the Negro national anthem. Understanding the divergent past of the United States of America between Blacks and Whites, Hunt wrote the *Community Anthem Song* as a pathway to conflict resolution over a matter that has been contended for decades. In an internal report for a mentoring and educational program called *The Akili Project A Celebration of Knowledge* (2002), Hunt wrote:

> The "Community Anthem" song seeks to bridge the divide between these contending views. It is not written to replace either song as an anthem. It is written to point the way to the unity inherent in the National Anthem and is reflective of the equity cry as represented by the Negro National Anthem. It mirrors the Inclusive Community Building (ICB) principles of moving from diversity, to unity, to community. (p. 35)

Over the decades, the Community Anthem Song has been professionally recorded, used in numerous plays, and taught to hundreds of adolescents and adults in numerous programs, workshops, and conferences. Similarly, other songs have been written using the tenants of The Ellison Model as its roadmap in order to teach and reinforce the topic of community building, character development, and economic development. The song lyrics are as follows:

for everyone

Verse 1: Diversity

    I am Variety

    I keep company, with culturally different people

    I am open to all things

    You may know me, by one of my other names

    I'm known as a group, or division in classification

Chorus

    I can talk to you

    I can call on you

    I know that you'll be there throughout all time I can walk with you

    I'd climb the great wall for you

    We are building community

Verse 2: Unity

    I am oneness

    I am of the same kind

    Though my color, age, and gender may differ

    Think of me, as total harmony

    Based on a set of beliefs that respects the right ways of life

Chorus

Verse 3: Community

    I am fellowship

    I enjoy working with others

    I am willing to break bread and share a drink with you

    My goal is inclusive,

    An omnipresent communion where things are held in common

    My desire is for mankind

Chorus (Repeat 2x)

for everyone

Article of Character

The following poem was originally written to serve as the creed of the Cordele Youth Summer Institute (CYSI), a character development program for middle and high school students in Cordele, Georgia. CYSI was founded and managed by Alicia Ritchey, Ed. D. as part of her dissertation research utilizing The Ellison Model. The poem was written to help reinforce positive values in a community known to have a high poverty and unemployment rate. Penned by Alicia Ritchey and me, the poem Article of Character (Carter, 2014) summarizes the intent of this book for emerging leaders, mentors, advisors, and supervising managers. The poem is a sustainable-teachable gesture that serves as a creed for inclusive community living and building. The poem states:

I recognize we're all a part of the community of life
I choose to build upon that legacy by doing what's just and right
Whatever the situation or even hesitation
Still I am a reflection of Goma's preparation

My attitude speaks of triumphs and success
Positioned to withstand and stand against any test
Understanding that challenges will arrive at my front door
My Attitude says, "Here is an opportunity for me to grow more"

So I'm left with no choice but to conduct myself
With humility and a greater sense of self
And this goes beyond playing the hand I was dealt
For I demonstrate behaviors that represent my wealth
I'm dedicated to the cause with a willingness to help
Myself help you so we both are helped

Speaking love to my neighbor with words that uplift
A genuine smile seeing the beauty and the gift
As a united existence of me and you
Caring, sharing, loving I'm commissioned to do
Let me count, reflect, and communicate the ways

In which our words create a brighter day to day

Tomorrow the process starts over again
We'll be ready and willing in a mode of discipline
To advance the cause and include even more
And by the end of that day be stronger than before

For indeed we are connected, part of the same beginning and end
From diversity to unity, no more strangers but friends.

CONCLUSION

Throughout the previous chapters we have discussed leadership in several relevant ways including,

- Leadership as the organization of survival,
- Leadership as an organism found in the individual in need of a proper host for growth and development,
- Leadership as a conglomerate of skills, and
- Leadership as a bridge between a problem and solution or conflict and resolution

We discussed the various concepts found within The Ellison Model, including

- The Five Foci, which are inclusion, multicultural appreciation, mentorship, conflict resolution, and relationship building,
- The Vectors of Diversity, Perspectives, and Potential Conflict
- The Inclusive Community-Discommunity Circular Diagram, and
- GOMABCD 7-Step Process
- Hunt's Theorem

We introduced new concepts adapted from The Ellison Model, including:

- TEM Principles Associative Graph
- Cole's Leadership-Solution Bridge, and
- Hunt's Experiential Leadership Process, dubbed The HELP.

for everyone

We also supported the theoretical framework and concepts of The Ellison Model, and the definitions of leadership with first-hand anecdotal scenarios and testimonials from professionals and students who have utilized The Model to guide aspects of their lives. All of this has been done to promote introspection, in some ways provide affirmation, and most importantly provide people of all ages, color, and creed a guided approach in being the right person, in the right place, at the right time by having a disposition of heart that aligns with The Ellison Model's inclusive community building tenets.

While much has been discussed, The Ellison Model is a life-long learning utility of the leadership development process. Noting about it happens overnight. Mistakes will be made along the way. Unexpected disruptions to your life plans will happen. You will not always know the unexpected to even expect the unexpected. It is a journey that all humans travel, whether educated on the process in the ways described in this book or not. It is sometimes a beautiful ugly, other times a cinematic marathon of everything going right, and other times a drift at sea that makes you question your final destination. But each moment teaches us valuable lessons. And through your inner-development, you are able to find the pearl in each ugly, in each frame, and in each lull of the life-long learning process. Time ultimately has the final say. Over time, we see that all things, in its due time, reveals itself in a timely fashion.

#

ABOUT THE AUTHOR

Adrian N. Carter has been impacting corporations, governmental entities, and institutions of higher education for over 16 years with his dynamic and progressive ability to lead, resolve conflict, and create solutions.

As a conflict resolution practitioner, keynote speaker, author, international spoken word artist, poet, and leadership development coach with a master's degree in higher education leadership, Adrian is committed to influencing people through his training, publications, and poetry into becoming more caring, sharing, and loving individuals who understand the importance of inclusive community building. Adrian is also pursuing his doctorate degree in conflict analysis and resolution.

Adrian's professional experiences with institutions of higher education, both as a student leader and a higher education administrator, have given him a first-hand understanding of both the desires and challenges institutions of higher education face. As a former Student Government President for two consecutive terms at Florida International University (FIU), Adrian is thankful for the opportunity that came under his presidency to lead a team that was directly responsible for allocating $7 million dollars to Student Affairs departments and programs, raising funds for international students, and helping welcome Division 1 football to FIU. Adrian also served as a member of FIU's Board of Directors. The impact Adrian N. Carter had on the department of Multicultural Programs and Services and Student Government propelled him into a professional career in Student Affairs for over 16 years, where he served as a higher education administrator in the roles of: Director of the Department of Student Life & Leadership Development; Associate Registrar/Student Records Administrator; Advisor to student leadership development organizations; and Adjunct faculty member.

Through his leadership development trainings, which empowers every individual to be the right person, in the right place, at the right time via The Ellison Model, developed by Adrian's mentor, world-class sociologist and professor Dr. Deryl G. Hunt, Adrian travels the world teaching leaders that "It's not the problem that counts, it's the solution."

Adrian N. Carter is your solution expert, calibrated for leadership in the 21st century with integrity and a deep care for teaching, learning, and approaching the social world with renewed ideas for inclusive community building.

ABOUT THE EDITOR

Dr. Alicia D. Ritchey emerges as a product of entrepreneurial heritage—both her parents were successful business proprietors. She is an educator, publisher, consultant, professional writer, public speaker, and program developer. A graduate of Florida International University (Miami, FL), Alicia received her Doctorate in Curriculum & Instruction, English Education. Her groundbreaking research resulted in a national curriculum for helping to develop classroom educators as character educators.

As a National Board Certified Teacher, the highest commendation for educators throughout the U.S., Alicia held numerous posts with Miami-Dade County Public Schools, including Instructor of English, Reading, and Creative Writing, Writing Coach & Professional Development Facilitator. An acclaimed international educator, she has done education consulting for the Bahamian government both in Nassau and Freeport, as well as the Turks and Caicos government.

Presently, she serves as a consultant for ICB Productions, Inc., an international education, research, and management firm. Given her long-time affiliations with ICB Productions, Alicia has been instrumental in developing programs and training material used in education, business, government, and faith-based sectors, making her a leading expert in inclusive community building affairs. She also serves as President/CEO of A Ritch Enterprise, LLC, specializing in small business and education consulting, editorial services, and event management, where her consulting services are in frequent demand. Inspired by her business mentor, Dr. Deryl G. Hunt, Alicia is known as a literary artisan and considered a word architect. A community building enthusiast, who is no stranger to mass communications, Alicia launched indigoLife™ Communications, Inc., Publisher of indigoLife™ Magazine, the nation's premiere magazine for inclusive community building, that showcases trailblazers from Middle and South Georgia, and abroad, whose lives are used as portraits of hope for the marginalized and the underserved.

Dr. Alicia Ritchey possesses a rich professional history that speaks to her character, creditability, and viability as a progressive educator, well-seasoned program developer, and savvy business leader of the 21st Century.

ACKNOWLEDGMENTS

Much thanks is owed to my mentor Deryl G. Hunt, Ph.D., who I have known since the age of seven. Dr. Hunt is a sociologist, higher education/Student Affairs administrator, college professor, author, playwright, and minister. For over three decades he has mentored a group of professionals who have gone on to assume high-level positions in various sectors. He's demonstrated an apt ability to be provocative, introspective, and groundbreaking. Growing up under his tutelage has proven immensely purposeful for me as I have gained exposure to the performing arts, learned how to critically think, research, write, and afforded international training and speaking opportunities through his company ICB Productions, Inc. As a fellow social scientist, my goal is to continue building on the work Dr. Hunt has started, specifically in deconstructing our social world and presenting renewed solutions that meet the needs of our time.

Thank you to Dr. Alicia Ritchey, John Harvey, Dawn Burgher, Donavan Burgher, Deryl G. Hunt, II, Sharonda Richardson, Adejare A. McMillan, Shaena Robinson, Wendy Heinzel, Miriam Deanna, Betzy Charles, Ayesha Williams, Cache Daily, Sharonda Richardson, and Lizz Florival for your contribution as readers of the original manuscript. Your feedback helped to make this book better.

Thank you to some very special people including my friend and colleague Laura Antzcak, my manager Marlene Bryan, Adnie Gaudin, Quadeera Teart, Danie Spikes, Ricky Lebrun, Moses Washington, Tracey Vincent, Adejare McMillan, Edwin Shepherd, Kenasha Paul, Felicia Martin, Lincoln Bain, and Simmone Bowe—many of the opportunities to speak and spread my wings as an entrepreneur in various capacities has been because of you.

Thank you to Nona Jones for your passion and commitment to lessening the knowledge and technology gap for the next generation. You are certainly a beacon of the community. I hope one day that you run for President of the United States of America.

A special thank you is owed to Dr. Mark Rosenberg and his continued mentorship. I am forever grateful for his support and interest in my success as an educator, conflict resolution practitioner, leadership development trainer, and higher education professional. Further thanks is owed to my overall student life experience at Florida International University and the plethora of people who contributed to it including former University President Modesto Maidique. My interactions with him, while I was as a student leader, gave me something to aspire toward. I am also thankful for Student Affairs professional Rafael Zapata and my student counterparts who contributed to a paradigm-shifting experience.

References

Allen, T. D., & Eby L. T. (2010). The Blackwell Handbook of Mentoring: A Multiple Perspectives Approach. Oxford, UK: Blackwell Publishing, pp. 7.

Astin, A. W. (1984). Student Involvement: A Developmental Theory for Higher Education. (Originally published 1984, Graduate School of Education, University of California). Journal of College Student Development Sept/Oct 1999, 40(5).

Bain, Read. (1928). An attitude on attitude research. American Journal of Sociology, 33, 940-957.

Carter, A. (2014). Lovebook II: perfectly joined together in the same mind and in the same poetry. Miami, FL: ICB Productions, Inc.

Chickering, A.W. (1969). Education and identity. San Francisco: Jossey-Bass. Chickering, A. W., Jon, J. C., Stamm, L (2006). Encouraging Authenticity and Spirituality in Higher Education. San Francisco: Jossey-Bass.

Chickering, A.W. & Reisser, L. (1993). Education and identity (2nd ed.). San Francisco: Jossey-Bass.

De Saussure, F. (1906-1911). Arbitrary Social Values and the Linguistic Sign. In Lemert, C. (Eds.), Social Theory The Multicultural, Global, and Classic Readings (119). Philadelphia: Westview Press.

DuBois, D. L., Holloway, B. E., Valentine J. C., & Cooper, H. (2002). Effectiveness of mentoring programs for youth: A meta-analytical review. American Journal of Community Psychology, 30, 157-197.

Ellison, H. Y. (2002). The efficacy of The Ellison Model as a retention initiative for first semester freshmen. Miami, FL: ProQuest ETD Collection for FIU. Paper AAI3049781.

Evans, N. J., Forney, D. S., & Guido-DiBrito, F. (1998). Student development in college: Theory, research, and practice. San Francisco: Jossey-Bass.

Fisher, N. I., and Nair, V. N. (2009). Quality management and quality practice: Perspectives on their history and their future. Applied Stochastic Models In Business And Industry Appl. Stochastic Models Bus. Ind. 2009; 25:1–28.

Frank, G. (2017, June 1). After 4-year-old girl's death, a reminder of cold water shock. Today.com. Retrieved from http://www.today.com/health/after-cold-water-shock-kills-teen-boy-his-mother-speaks-t98276.

Galtung, J. (1969). Violence, Peace, and Peace Research. Journal of Peace Research, 6 (3), 167-191.

Hocker, J. and Wilmot. W. (2014) Interpersonal Conflict. New York: McGraw-Hill.

Hoyt, D. J. (2013). Living Two Lives: The Ability Of Low Income African American Females In Their Quest To Break The Glass Ceiling Of Education Through The Ellison Model (Tem) Mentoring Approach. ProQuest: Washington State University, 2013, 167; 3587106.

Hunt, D. G. (2000a). Community Moments & Teachable Seconds. Retrieved from The ICB International Library at http://thelawofnaturalanointing.com/usc.html.

Hunt, D. G. (2000b). The Foundation for Building the Inclusive Community. Retrieved from The ICB International Library at http://thelawofnaturalanointing.com/usc.html.

Hunt, D. G. (2002). The Akili Project A Celebration of Knowledge. An internal report and one-act play. Miami, FL: ICB Productions, Inc.

Hunt, D. G. (2003). Presentation on Conflict Resolution. Retrieved from The ICB International Library at http://thelawofnaturalanointing.com/usc.html.

Hunt, D. G. (2006a). 7 Steps to Character Development. The ICB Character Education & Community Building Book Series, Meet Goma. Retrieved from The ICB International Library at http://thelawofnaturalanointing.com/Education/Training/7%20Steps%20to%20Character%20Development2.pdf

Hunt, D. G. (2006b). The ICB Character Education & Community Building Book Series, A is for Attitude. Retrieved from The ICB International Library at http://thelawofnaturalanointing.com/Education/Books/A%20is%20for%20Attitude.pdf

Hunt, D. G. (2007). The ABCD's of Urban Renewal. Retrieved from The ICB International Library at http://thelawofnaturalanointing.com/Government/Training/The_ABCD'S_OF_URBAN_RENEWAL.pdf

Hunt D. G. and Hunt, D. (2008) The ABCDs of Schizophrenic Community Building Character Development. Retrieved from The ICB International Library at http://thelawofnaturalanointing.com/Education/Training/Schizo_Little_Book_Mini_Version.pdf

Hunt, D. G. (2008). Report at 5th International Globalization, Diversity, & Education Conference. Washington State University. Spokane, WA.

Hunt, D. G. (2009) (2012). The Law of Natural Anointing. Miami, FL: ICB Productions, Inc.

Hunt, D.G. & Ritchey, A. (2000). The Ellison Model Techniques. Retrieved from http://thelawofnaturalanointing.com/Education/Training/EM%20Techniques.pdf

Jacobi, M. (1991). Mentoring and undergraduate academic success. A literature review. Review of Educational Research, 61, 505-532.

Kolb, D. A. (1981, 1985). Kolb's Cycle of Learning. Experienced-Based Learning Systems, Inc. 1981, revised 1985

Kolb, D. A. (1984). Experiential learning: Experience as the source of learning and development. Englewood Cliffs, NJ: Prentice Hall.

Kram, K. E. (1985). Mentoring at work: Developmental relationships at work. Glenview, IL: Scott, Foreman and Company.

Kuh, G. D., & Pike, G. R. (2005). A Typology Of Student Engagement For American Colleges And Universities. Research in Higher Education, 46(2), 185-209. Lemert, C. (2017). Social Theory The Multicultural, Global, and Classic Readings. Philadelphia: Westview Press.

Levinger, G. (1979). A Social Exchange View On The Dissolution Of Pair Relationships. In R. L. Burgess & T. L. Huston (Eds). Social exchange in developing relationships (pp. 169-196). New York: Academic Press.

Levinson, D. J., Darrow, D., Levinson, M., Klein, E. B. & McKee, B. (1978). The Seasons of a man's life. New York: Knopf.

Lewicki, R. J., & Bunker, B. B. (1995). Trust in relationships: A model of trust development and decline. In B. B. Bunker & J. Z. Rubin (Eds.), Conflict, cooperation, and justice (pp. 133-173). San Francisco: Jossey-Bass.

Marx, K. (1844). Estranged Labour. In Lemert, C. (Eds.), Social Theory The Multicultural, Global, and Classic Readings (29). Philadelphia: Westview Press. Maslow, A.H. (1987). Motivation and Personality. (3rd ed.). New York, NY: Harper & Row.

Maslow, A.H. (1999). Towards a Psychology of Being. (3rd ed.). New York, NY: John Wiley & Sons.

Northouse, Peter. (1997). Leadership: Theory and Practice. Thousand Oaks, CA: Sage Publications, Inc.

Park, M. and Fantz, A. (2010, October 26). Swimming in warm water can take deadly toll on body. CNN.com. Retrieved from http://www.cnn.com/2010/HEALTH/10/25/swim.temperature.factors/

Thomas, W.I. and Znaniecki, F. (1918). The Polish Peasant in Europe and America. Boston, Gorham Press.

Rice, C. M. (2001). A Case Study of the Ellison Model's Use of Mentoring as an Approach Toward Inclusive Community Building. Miami, FL: ProQuest ETD Collection for FIU. Paper AAI3015938, 79.

Rice, C. M. (2007). Newsletter on The Economic Empowerment Through Community Building Conference in Freeport, Bahamas, pp 2.

Rice, C. M. & Rice, M. (2012). Conflict resolution and the Scholarship of Engagement: Partnerships transforming conflict. In C. L. Duckworth & C. Kelley (Eds.), Newcastle upon Tyne, Great Britain: Cambridge Scholars Publishing.

Ritchey, A. D. (2012). Goma Curriculum, A Character Education Paradigm: Composing a Text for Shaping Classroom Character Culture. Miami, FL: ProQuest ETD Collection for FIU. Paper AAI3554203, pp 146.

Forgette, R., Dettrey, B., Van Boening, M., Swanson, D. A. (2011). Before, Now, and After: Assessing Hurricane Katrina Relief. Published online: 12 November 2008. Ó Springer Science+Business Media B.V. 2008.

Robinson, M. (2015). Fear. In Lemert, C. (Eds.), Social Theory The Multicultural, Global, and Classic Readings (533). Philadelphia: Westview Press.

Rendon, L. I. (1994). Validating culturally diverse students: Toward a new model of learning and student development Innovative Higher Education, 19, 33-51.

Ramsbotham, O., Woodhouse, T., and Miall, H. (2011) Contemporary Conflict Resolution. Malden, MA: Polity.

Sanford, N. (1966) (2009). Self and Society: Social Change and Individual Development. New Jersey: Transaction Publishers.

Sanford, N. (1969). Why Colleges Fail. San Fransisco: Jossey-Bass.

Scandura, T. A., & Pellegrini, E. K. (2003, November). A multidimensional model of trust and LMX. Southern Management Association Meeting, Clearwater Beach, FL.

Schlossberg, N. (1989). Marginality and Mattering: Key Issues in Building Community. New Directions for Student Services, No. 48.

Spotting (Weight training). In Wikipedia. Retrieved from https://en.wikipedia.org/wiki/Spotting_(weight_training))

Symonds, P.M. (1925). A Social-Attitudes Questionnaire. Journal of Educational Psychology, pp. 316-22.